Solving
Elk Hunting Problems

SIMPLE SOLUTIONS TO THE ELK HUNTING RIDDLE

MIKE LAPINSKI

SOLVING
ELK HUNTING PROBLEMS

SIMPLE SOLUTIONS TO THE ELK HUNTING RIDDLE

Mike Lapinski

Copyright 2002 by Mike Lapinski

Published in the United States of America

Library of Congress Card Number 2002109629

ISBN 1-931291-19-5 (softcover)
ISBN 1-931291-20-9 (hardcover)

First Edition

STONEYDALE PRESS PUBLISHING COMPANY
523 Main Street • P.O. Box 188
Stevensville, Montana 59870
Phone: 406-777-2729

Table of Contents

Introduction

SOLVING ELK HUNTING PROBLEMS

This book will help you identify and quickly solve any given problem during your elk hunt, because we don't live in a perfect world where every bull comes running in to an elk call. No matter how much we prepare ourselves, an elk has a way of altering our best laid plans. A bull may hang up just out of range, or retreat. Another bull might clam up and come in silently, or slip away without notice. Do these elk represent lost opportunities? No way! There are hunting techniques – some proven, others newly discovered – and some still experimental – that are covered in this book to help you turn these seemingly lost causes into trophies on the wall.

My first elk book, *Radical Elk Hunting Strategies*, has become the bible for aggressive archery elk hunters. But I also admit that the elk herd has evolved over the years, and new elk calls and techniques have been discovered to help the aggressive bowhunter better deal with the unexpected. Hence, the first chapter of this book addresses the need to look at aggressive (radical) elk hunting from an evolving perspective. Whether you are a bow or rifle hunter, this chapter on aggressive elk hunting is a must.

Are elk really becoming smarter? They certainly don't come waltzing in to an elk call like they used to! But are they actually smarter? I say no, but they have changed – in many ways for the better – as habitat changes and hunting pressure impacts their lives, and I'll discuss these positive and negative influences on today's elk herd in the second chapter titled, "Solving Today's Educated Elk."

My many years of observing rutting elk have given me a thorough understanding of the elk's mating cycle. After intensely studying how an elk reacts to the calls of nearby rutting elk, I've developed a deadly calling method called, "Peak Rut Elk Calling," which simulates the excited calling of both cows and bulls during the peak of the rut. This method is fully explained in chapter three.

So how do you hunt today's elk? The answer is to use proven elk hunting methods, but for those situations that cry for "something different" I have great news! The fourth chapter of this book explains some new and experimental elk hunting methods and calls that are soon to become standard items in every successful elk bowhunters arsenal, such as decoying, rattling, glunking, etc.

Unfortunately, many of our elk hunting endeavors are haunted by wasted opportunities – those instances when a careless move, or a swirl of the wind, defeats us. It is vital that we learn from our failures, and the errors of others, so we can avoid these silly mistakes that doom an elk

hunt, often times before it even begins. For that reason, I've dedicated an entire chapter to wasted opportunities and how to avoid them.

But this is primarily a book about solving problems. What's the best way to hunt the early season? How do you draw in that hung up bull those last twenty yards into bow range? Can you realistically expect to get within bow range of a retreating bull? Is there any hope when that big old herd bull continues pushing his cows away from you? And what's the secret to provoking a silent bull to sound off? All these questions and more will be addressed, dissected and solved in separate chapters.

Every year frustrated bowhunters share with me sad tales of elk shot and lost. The good news is that there are answers to the following questions: What is a proper elk shot? How do you find a bowshot bull? These questions will be addressed in separate chapters in this book and should be required reading for any ethical bowhunter because the bull elk presents specific shot selection and blood trailing problems.

My last chapter, "The Philosophy of Elk Hunting Today," may be the most important to the future of elk hunting because it explores where we, as elk lovers and sportsmen, are headed with elk hunting. There are some positive – and some very negative – issues looming. So vital, in fact, are these issues that our attention to them (or lack of) may very well tip the balance of future elk hunting either way.

Elk are beautiful animals, mighty in stature and magnificent to behold as their roam through their pristine wilderness lairs. But elk are also complicated animals, and so are the issues surrounding them. This book is dedicated to solving all of them.

Good Hunting!

Mike Lapinski
Superior, Montana
June 3, 2002

The accepted, but erroneous, elk hunting theory when I first began bowhunting elk 35 years ago was that any archer who perfectly simulated a rutting elk's bugle could bring in a bull

Chapter 1

RADICAL ELK HUNTING – AN EVOLVING CONCEPT

The Radical Elk Hunting Strategy, perfected by me twenty years ago, has revolutionized the way bowhunters pursue rutting bull elk. An entire generation of archery hunters has used the aggressive (radical) method of hunting to change their fortunes for the better. Instead of hiding behind a bush hundreds of yards away from a bugling bull and tooting on a bugle, hoping some bull might have pity and come waltzing in, these courageous archers move in and confront that rutting bull, forcing him to either put up or shut up.

The proof of their success comes from hundreds of phone calls and letters with trophy photos I've received from appreciative bowhunters who inform me that my book, *Radical Elk Hunting Strategies,* has helped them move up from empty handed frustration to scoring consistently with elk.

I know how it feels to be a frustrated elk hunter. I discovered the Radical Elk Hunting Strategy almost thirty years ago because I was unhappy with my mediocre success of one bull and a cow. I was confused about the rut and the proper way to hunt rutting bulls, and I had grave reservations about the accepted elk hunting theory back then – that any archer who perfectly simulated a rutting elk's bugle could bring in a bull.

You have to remember that back in the 1970's we had none of the modern elk bugles of today. Our calls were homemade flute-like contraptions made with a foot-long length of plastic hose and notched plug in one end, and they sounded nothing like a bull elk's bugle.

After several frustrating elk encounters, I traveled to Yellowstone National Park to study rutting bull elk and hopefully find some answers. My first eye-opener occurred one morning while I listened to three bugling bulls, each located in pockets of timber about 200 yards apart near a large meadow. Real bulls were bugling at each other, yet I witnessed no confrontations. It became obvious to me that the tired old theory that good bugling brought in bulls on the run was erroneous because these bulls were screaming at each other without fighting.

As I watched this confusing scenario, another bull came over a low ridge and passed within sixty yards of where one of the bulls was holed up. When the wayward bull bugled, the resident bull erupted with frenzied bugling and immediately charged forward to confront the trespassing bull. The resident bull raked his antlers in the grass, tore up trees and screamed at the offending bull until it moved off.

Aha! I thought. Maybe bulls don't want to fight each other after all. Maybe they're simply prone to aggressively confront intruders. After watching two similar incidents the next day, I left for my home in Idaho, excited to try my new elk hunting theory.

It didn't take long to get results. At first light atop a lonely ridge in North Idaho's Clearwater River country, I bugled and immediately got a response from a bull on a distant ridge. We called back and forth for a half hour, and it became obvious that the bull had no intention of tromping down the deep canyon and then all the way up the other side to get to me.

It was time to test my radical new elk hunting theory. I stopped bugling and skidded a thousand feet down to the stream bottom, then started up the other side. The bull's occasional bugling allowed me to keep his location pinpointed. I sneaked to the edge of a fern glade, but dared not advance farther for fear of being spotted by the bull. (A rutting bull will run off at the sight or smell of man.)

I sucked in a deep, ragged breath and bugled. A deathly silence enveloped the mountainside, and I was beginning to wonder if my theory was bogus, when the bull erupted with a furious bugle. I could hear him tearing at the brush and raking his antlers on trees. I took that opportunity to move up to the edge of an alder thicket, and I bugled again. That bull bugled with as much emotion as I've ever heard in the elk woods.

A jolt of adrenalin shot through me as hooves pounded on the forest floor and brush snapped just out of sight. The bull appeared like an apparition – head back, large chocolate brown antlers swept back, ivory tips gleaming in the morning sun. When the massive animal disappeared behind a screen of trees, I hastily raised my bow and drew back. The bull broke into the open just ten yards away, blazing red eyes searching the fern glade below for the brazen imp who'd dared invade his domain.

Radical elk hunting relies on confrontation as its main tool. When surprised by a bugle at close range, most bulls will come forward in anger, frustration, or curiosity to check out the strange bull in their domain.

My arrow zipped forward and buried fletch-deep in the bull's chest. He charged off, and a deathly silence enveloped the forest. A loud, hollow cough floated back through the crisp mountain air, then another and another, followed by a loud crash. A few minutes later I stared in awe at the large five-point bull lying at my feet – my first bowkilled elk using the Radical Elk Hunting Strategy.

Simply put, the Radical Elk Hunting Strategy recognizes the rutting bull elk as a territorial animal that goes through somewhat of a mating ritual. When confronted by an intruder into his domain, he tears up brush and trees and bugles out a challenge and warning that he is the biggest, baddest bull in the woods. With that done, he feels justified and usually stomps off. Actual combat between rutting bulls is rare.

Radical elk hunting relies on confrontation as its main tool. Think about it. Isn't that what any bugling bull is doing? He is confronting an adversary, real or imagined, and warning him to stay away. At long range, a bull is content to scream out his disdain, but move in close, literally to his back door, and he is forced to flee or fight. Most bulls, when surprised by a bugle at close range, will come forward in anger, frustration or curiosity to at least check out who the strange bull is in their domain.

Just remember, things happen fast with a radical challenge. After you move in close to a bull and challenge him, it's often just a few seconds before that bull is broadside at close range. I always seek a good ambush point and hide, then nock an arrow and have my bow up and ready before bugling.

One of the best things about Radical Elk Hunting is that you don't need a Ph.D. in "Elkology" to make it work. Several years ago I invited three Wisconsin men to join me on an elk archery hunt through the North American Hunting Club's Swap Hunt program. My plan was to hunt along with these men, but good fortune intervened. I killed a dandy five-point bull on September first, opening day of Idaho's elk archery season. Montana's archery season opened the next Saturday, and I killed a 5X6 bull the first morning. So when the three Wisconsin men arrived on the 10th of September, my elk tags were filled, but they sure got an eyeful when I showed them exactly what the Radical Elk Hunting Strategy could accomplish.

The men were enthusiastic, but woefully lacking in elk knowledge, so I sat them down around a campfire and explained the radical elk hunting concept. I told them that, even if they didn't know a lot about elk, they could still be successful if they followed my instructions.

I gave them a day to stretch their legs and set up camp. On the second morning, I took Jim Kingsley with me to the Idaho/Montana border. As we hiked along a ridge covered with frost-burnt huckleberry bushes, I explained where to look for elk and how to hunt them. As I was instructing him, a bull bugled from a distant ridge. Jim asked, "What about that bull? Is he too far away, or is there any chance I could get in on him?"

I grinned and nodded in the direction of the bull. "Let's go find out."

After a half hour of steadily moving toward the bugling bull, we cautiously advanced to the crest of a sharp ridge. The bull bugled, and I pinpointed his location in a stand of spruce trees about sixty yards to our right. I waited until Jim hid behind a clump of mountain maple bushes, then I bugled. A quick bugle ripped through the air, but to our left. Before we could change positions, a bull broke cover and trotted at us. It wasn't the bull from the thicket, but a smaller satellite bull that had been lurking nearby. The bull stood fifteen yards away staring at Jim, but winded us and ran off.

The author congratulates Jim Kingsley with his big 6X7 bull, taken using the Radical Elk Hunting Method.

I frantically motioned Jim to move up and we scooted forward another twenty yards before setting up again. Now, we were only forty yards from the bull in the spruce thicket. I bugled and the bull screamed back a reply. We moved up another ten yards, and I bugled again. The bull stomped forward and stood in a small opening thirty yards away, angrily seeking his challenger. Jim rose up and sent an arrow deep into the bull's chest. The elk stumbled, regained his legs, and crashed through the brush. After a half hour wait and a short search, we found Jim's bull. He was a magnificent 6X7 bull that scored over 300 points, well above the minimum for the Pope & Young record book.

As we sat around the campfire that night, Jim's told me that our hunt had been successful beyond his wildest dreams. "Oh by the way," he added, "your radical elk hunting method really works." The other two men didn't fare too badly, either. A few days later they collected a five-point bull and a cow.

As successful as the Radical Elk Hunting concept has been through the years, there have been times when this particular method did not work for me. When, for whatever reason, a bull that is confronted in his own back yard at close range decides to retreat, rather than investigate. Other archers have also experienced this perplexing phenomenon, leading some skeptics to wonder aloud that maybe the Radical Elk Hunting Strategy is outdated. "After all," they point out, "we've got so many new elk calls and hunting techniques nowadays that we can throw a lot more at a rutting bull."

"Yeah," I usually reply, "but not if you're hiding behind a skinny little sapling 400 yards away." In other words, radical elk hunting employs a single hunting method – confronting a bull in his domain – but it is the philosophy of radical (aggressive) hunting that is the prime ingredient in most successful elk archery hunts. You can take to the woods with the hottest new elk call and a ton of elk savvy, but you're not going to do any good if you don't stride forward and present your ruse to that bull elk in his home range where he feels comfortable.

The Radical Elk Hunting Strategy remains the most successful hunting tactic for experienced bowhunters, and every serious elk hunter should consider picking up a copy of the book. Order information can be found on Page 190.

However, it would be arrogant and misleading of me to claim it's the only way to hunt rutting elk. Even the best elk hunter carries more than one arrow in his quiver, just in case, and he also brings additional elk hunting methods to the field because, as I mentioned, nothing works all the time. But something new just might.

In the coming chapters, you'll learn about these new and exciting elk hunting calls and tactics, but remember, an aggressive (radical) approach remains the vital ingredient, whether you're trying a glunking call, a hot new estrus cow call, or decoying or rattling – you name it.

Bowhunters using the Radical Elk hunting Strategy have accounted for many thousands of successful bowhunts. But rather than fade away as an archaic method of yesteryear, it has evolved because it is based on a sound biological principle of aggression. And aggression, my friend, is what the elk rut is all about.

The key to successfully hunting today's educated elk is to understand how they have adapted to their mountain homes by altering their habits.

Chapter 2

SOLVING TODAY'S EDUCATED ELK

A fellow walked up to me after one of my elk seminars and asked, "Why didn't you talk about how smart elk are today?" The guy shook his head and continued, "The elk around here don't even bugle anymore because of all the hunters calling at them and educating them. Now they clam up when you bugle. Ya gotta hunt 'em like deer anymore."

I hear this lament from at least a hundred bowhunters every year – that elk have become too smart to call in. They reply that bulls who once came in to a bugle, now sulk away, or stop calling. And at times during the rut, they add, bugling actually ceases, which these frustrated bowhunters claim is proof that the elk have wised up.

You couldn't tell by recent elk harvest statistics. From a massive herd of almost a million animals, hunters have killed almost two hundred thousand elk annually, making today's take among of the largest harvests ever recorded.

I'm in the elk woods through the entire hunting season. And when I'm not hunting elk, I'm studying them. I don't believe that the elk have become smarter; they've just changed their habits in response to the encroachment of civilization, be it in the form of more roads and rural subdivisions, or increased hunting pressure

We have to remember that an elk is an animal, and therefore incapable of reasoning. An elk just reacts instinctively to situations it encounters. For instance, a bull is not capable of sizing up a distant bugle and wondering, "Is that a real elk calling at me, or is it a bowhunter?"

However, that same bull will become much more wary and careful if it has been chased by predators, such as a pack of wolves. And it will also become much more tentative after a few bad experiences with bowhunters. Heck, elk even act that way among themselves. More than once I've watched a young bull, called a raghorn, get pummeled by the big herd bull after it got too close to the cows. Thereafter, any nearby bugle would send the young bull hastily retreating over the ridge.

Consequently, those areas with a lot of hunting pressure are sure to harbor elk that tend to be more wary, especially after they've responded to a call and saw or smelled a human. A simple bugle from a ridge top is not going to prompt such a bull to come on the run because the last time that particular bull responded to a call, it encountered a smelly bowhunter hiding behind a tree on the upwind side of the trail.

So does all this mean that elk have quit bugling, opting instead to perform their rutting rituals as mutes? Absolutely not! Elk country is too big for the bulls to locate cows strung out through hundreds of square miles of rugged habitat. Instead, a bull elk depends upon the excited bugles of other bulls to clue him in that a cow is in heat, because the first bull that sniffs her will start bugling up a storm. This is the way a bull elk locates hot cows, whether it's in the heart of Oregon's Eagle Cap Wilderness, or the brushy fringes a few miles from Portland.

The adaptability of the elk should not surprise us because this animal has been adapting for hundreds of years as it slowly retreated from the onslaught of civilization. Once abundant in all the eastern, southern, and midwestern states, the elk was decimated by colonists with flintlocks who killed it for its tasty meat while uprooting its prime habitat.

By the time Lewis and Clark embarked on their epic journey west, the elk had been extirpated east of the Mississippi. Lewis and Clark discovered vast herds of buffalo living on the Great Plains, but they also spotted large herds of elk living quite comfortably in this endless sea of grass.

Market hunters and settlers exterminated the buffalo, who failed to adapt to the meager forage in the dense forests. The elk, on the other hand, easily adapted to the more austere conditions in the mountains, quickly learning to slip into lush openings to feed at night, and then retreating into their timbered lairs before dawn to escape the guns of daylight.

Today, elk are doing the same thing. They're adapting. It should not surprise us when the bulls in a particular drainage who were, at first, easy to lure in to bow range even using crude elk calls, eventually adapt to the threat and become more wary and difficult to fool.

The key to successfully hunting today's educated (adapted) elk is to understand why and how they've altered their habits. With this understanding, you'll be able to devise exciting new hunting methods that the elk haven't been exposed to yet. And by the time they wise up to those tricks, you'll have moved on to even newer calls and hunting methods.

Those areas with a lot of hunting pressure are sure to harbor elk that tend to be more wary, especially after they've responded to a call and seen or smelled a human.

Why Elk Have Altered Their Habits

When left alone, elk exist under natural herd conditions. An elk herd in the heart of the wilderness is a good example. In those areas where hunting pressure is low or nonexistent, the biggest bulls round up cows and jealously defend their harems. Lonely bachelor bulls, mature and fully capable of mating, roam the outskirts of the elk herd, itching to take out their frustrations on any bull foolish enough to get in their way.

When I travel to Canada's Banff National Park to photograph elk in September, I observe mature bachelor bulls pummeling each other in frustration and rage, while the herd bull and his harem look on from a distance. Of course, the younger bulls, four-points and smaller five-points, squeak out an occasional bugle, but are careful to avoid sounding off too much or they'll end up with a big bachelor bull's antlers rammed up their butts.

These back country areas where natural herd conditions exist are the places I seek when I bowhunt because when I give a toot on a bugle, that nearby bachelor bull is going to react quickly and aggressively to

Elk rut and bugle as much as ever in those areas lacking heavy hunting pressure.

vanquish his unseen tormentor. Some of these areas are true wilderness that I hike into and set up a spike camp. This type of hunting, in my opinion, is the most enjoyable way to spend those balmy Indian Summer days in the elk woods. It is not unusual for me to bring in a half dozen bulls each day in these areas because the elk simply are not accustomed to a bowhunter's calling.

However, natural herd conditions also exist closer to access roads than most sportsmen realize, like in the bottom of that deep draw off the end of a road where guys joke about needing a frying pan to hunt the place – meaning it's too tough to haul a bull out. That's nonsense, especially if you know how to no-mess field dress an elk. (Refer to Chapter 10 of my book, *High Pressure Elk Hunting,* to learn about this critically important method of removing the meat from an elk without gutting it. It'll stretch your hunting range an extra two miles into the back country.)

Last year in Montana I experienced frantic bugling activity in three different areas that were within one mile of a driveable road, with upwards to five bulls screaming at me. These were brushy areas, or the bottoms of draws, that the lazy hunters drive past on their way to an easy trail or ridge top , where they saunter along in a vain search for an easy elk. These are the same guys who claim the elk have smartened up and quit bugling.

How Elk Have Altered Their Habits

In my opinion, bull elk today bugle as much as ever in those areas where natural herd conditions exist. The big bulls constantly scream out a warning to lesser bulls to stay away, or else. Mature bachelor bulls and younger raghorns scream back protests, while chasing each other through the elk woods.

But when roads are pushed into, or near, these formerly isolated areas, hunting pressure increases dramatically, and the mature trophy bull population is decimated. These are the older bulls who compete most intensely during the rut, even fighting to the death for the right to mate. When this intense competition ceases, so does the intense bugling. There simply is no reason for all that frantic calling among competing bulls. In some areas where elk numbers are high, but bull numbers as low as five mature bulls per hundred cows, there is no need to bugle out a warning to other bulls to stay away – because they don't exist!

In addition, large harems of cows are gathered up by young bulls who have not yet developed the fiery rutting belligerence common among mature herd bulls. In those areas of Montana and Idaho where hunting pressure is heavy, I've observed raghorn bulls trying to act like herd bulls, each with their own harems of cows barely fifty yards away, with cows amiably passing back and forth! In a natural herd condition, those herd bulls would either fight to the death or stay far away from each other while screaming insults all day long.

Yet even in hard hunted areas, most of the cows are bred each year, and plenty of calves are born in the spring. The elk have simply adapted, with younger bulls now mating the cows. But what does change for worse, if you're a bowhunter, is the vocal nature of the fall elk rut. That natural herd condition, where mature bulls intensely rutted and bugled, doesn't exist anymore. And those young bulls who now do the mating just don't bugle as much.

The above description is typical elk country today. It's also the place where most bowhunters roam, frustrated because there are a lot of elk in the area, but the bulls don't bugle much, and rarely come in to their calling. And why should they? They already have what they want!

Two naturally occurring maladies also affect rutting activity, even where natural herd conditions exist. The first is the full phase of the

One of the reasons that the bulls may suddenly quit bugling at the peak of the rut is the presence of a full moon. The extra light allows the elk to rut hard all night, and by the time a bowhunter arrives in the area at first light, the elk are bedded for the day.

moon. I always look ahead on the calendar to see where the full moon falls in the month of September. A full moon early or late in the month usually means brisk evening and morning rut activity during its dark phase in mid-September. But a full moon rising over the elk woods during the mid-September peak of the rut bodes ill for the bowhunter.

That's because the normally dark forest is bathed in the full moon's eerie light, and the elk feed and rut hard all night, with nothing left for the prime morning and evening hours. A few years ago I sat in a tent in Colorado and listened every night to the maddening bugles of bulls, but at first light the next morning the forest would be silent. The bowhunters I encountered were dumbstruck by the absence of bugling right through the peak of the rut. Of course, they hadn't seen or heard what I had from my tent, and they fell back on the tired old excuse that the elk had wised up and quit bugling.

The second malady is the tentative nature of the elk rut. An elk herd becomes more vocal when a few cows enter their estrus period, normally the middle of September, but that time frame may vary two weeks either way. I've observed bulls screaming at each other in rutting lust the last week in August when a few cows went into heat early, but the next week the elk woods were silent, except for an occasional forlorn bugle because there were no hot cows to get the bulls fired up.

This ebb and flow of the elk rut is one of the great points of confusion for the average bowhunter, who may experience frantic elk activity for a day or two, but then the bugling dies off, and he mistakenly concludes that his improper calling is what shut the bulls up. But after the bowhunter gives up the hunt in disgust, a few more cows come in heat and the hills once again ring with elk bugles while he's at home complaining that the bulls "just don't bugle like they used to."

Let's face it, something must be going on in the elk woods because there's more elk than ever. The bulls continue with their mating rituals, impregnating thousands of cows each fall. As long as this drama unfolds each fall, a bowhunter should be able to take advantage of it.

I bowkill elk all the time, even in hard hunted areas, because I've developed an exciting new hunting method I call Peak Rut Elk Calling, which employs a new calling technique, a new hunting method, and the venerable radical (aggressive) hunting style. While other archers are sulking at home, complaining that the elk aren't bugling enough, I'm experiencing frenzied rutting activity. Whenever I invite one of these disgruntled bowhunters to accompany me, they are not only shocked by the frantic rutting action, but also encouraged because they realize that

Peak Rut Elk Calling is something they can do.

In summary, today's elk are more numerous than ever and just as huntable if you bring along new calling techniques and hunting methods, and a radical (aggressive) attitude.

Chapter 3

PEAK RUT ELK CALLING

Three days into the 1998 Colorado elk archery season, I met two bowhunters trudging along a forest trail in the Routt National Forest. The date was August 30th, just three days into elk archery season. Discouraged by the summer-like heat and lack of bugling activity, these men were packing out their camp and giving up the hunt.

I was similarly burdened, but with a pack frame loaded down with eighty pounds of fresh meat and an elk rack.

After staring open-mouthed at the large six-point rack, one the men asked, "How'd you get the bull? Did you hunt a wallow, or did you sit along a trail?"

"Naw," I gasped as I unburdened myself of the heavy pack frame. "I called him in."

"But how?" the other guy asked, a plaintive note in his voice. "We couldn't hardly get any bulls to bugle. They're just not real hot yet."

"I have a way to get the bulls fired up." I replied. "Have you ever heard of peak rut elk calling?" Both men stared blankly while shaking their heads. Whereupon we sat on a log and I explained to those men how to get those bulls fired up.

I've solved the problem of lethargic early season elk and reluctant mid-season bulls by developing an exciting new method called Peak Rut Elk Calling. And I must admit, I discovered it by accident. During my early years of elk archery hunting, I noticed with some degree of smugness that I was able to fire up the bulls and kill elk when other bowhunters could hardly even get the bulls to answer. For a while, I mistakenly thought that my exceptional calling was the reason for my success, but after listening to the superior calling ability of others, I had

I've solved the problem of lethargic early season elk and reluctant mid-season bulls by developing an exciting new method called Peak Rut Elk Calling.

to admit that I was, at best, an average caller. Which got me to wondering exactly what it was about my calling that got the bulls fired up, while other bowhunters were ignored.

The answer came while I was filming elk near the aptly-named Whistler Campground outside Jasper, British Columbia. The elk rut was in its early stages, with the bulls just beginning to bugle. On the second morning, I watched as a small bull pranced up to a cow, who stood with her rear legs slightly spread and butt raised. The bull sniffed the cow's rump and went wild, bellowing out a string of bugles. I counted six in one minute, then four, then five. Responding to this sudden outburst of bugles, bulls back in the timber began to bugle. Within a half hour, three other bulls, a four-point and two large five-points, had migrated to the source of the excitement – a single cow in heat. Finally, a huge six-point bull tromped out of a stand of lodgepole pine trees, quickly vanquished the lesser bulls with his aggressive posturing, and became the herd bull.

As I watched that amazing display of rutting activity, the thought struck me like a load of bricks: "That's what you're doing when you bugle. You're calling so much, that the bulls think there's a hot cow nearby." That, my friends, is how Peak Rut Elk Calling was born – by mistake!

I readily admit to being a type A personality. (My wife claims I'm hyper A!) I'm also a bit impatient, so if the bulls didn't bugle in the early season, I bugled and bugled and bugled and bugled until the bulls began returning my calls. I didn't realize it at the time, but they were responding to the quantity of my calls, not the quality. I was unwittingly fooling those lethargic bulls into thinking I was a bull who'd discovered a hot cow.

Understanding the Elk Rut

Understanding the dynamics of the elk rut makes Peak Rut Elk Calling easy to master. For eleven and a half months in the year, a bull elk is nothing more than a huge deer. Through the summer months, its antlers grow in a velvet sheath as it whiles away the lazy days of summer in a bachelor herd that often numbers a dozen bulls or more.

Toward the end of August a small amount of the male hormone, testosterone, is released into the bull's bloodstream from its testicles. It flows up to the base of the antlers and coagulates the capillaries that nourish them. These cartilage-like appendages soon die and quickly harden, whereupon the bull rubs the velvet off on a bush or tree sometime around the last week in August.

Toward the end of August, a small amount of the male hormone, testosterone, is released into a bull's bloodstream, which coagulates the arteries at the base of the antlers, thereby killing and hardening them. From that moment on, the bull is capable of mating.

At this point, a bull elk is biologically capable of mating (and being called in) because his body is manufacturing testosterone. (We human males have testosterone in our systems all the time.)

The problem is that cow elk usually don't enter their estrus cycles until the middle of September. And without the swollen vulva and necessary lubricating fluids that result when a cow elk enters her estrus cycle, mating is impossible. So a bull elk enters a mournful period of impatiently waiting for the nearby cows to come into heat. He bugles out an occasional bugle of frustration, which also serves notice to any cows in the area that he is ready and willing to mate.

Meanwhile, each bull continues to check out the cows in his area, sniffing the air for the tantalizing aroma of airborne pheromones. But the elk woods are too vast for a bull to check out every call, so he bugles out his mournful pleas and listens to the replies of other bulls to find out if there's a hot cow on a distant mountainside.

This is the period of time during the rut when most archery seasons open: the bulls are hard-horned and occasionally bugling, but rutting activity is almost nonexistent and may continue that way for days, even weeks. By adding their own periodic, timid bugles to the slumbering elk rut, bowhunters further hurt their cause by reminding the bulls in the area that nothing exciting is happening. Eventually, most bowhunters go home frustrated, doubting their calling ability and often drawing the erroneous conclusion that the bulls have wised up and become call-shy.

Eventually, a cow on some finger ridge enters her estrus cycles, and a nearby raghhorn bull catches a whiff of those tantalizing pheromones. Flicking out his tongue like a snake to taste the airborne pheromones, the young bull pursues the cow, erupting in furious, lust-driven bugling. Every bull within ear shot notices the sudden excitement in the raghorn's bugling. A certain number of bulls will move toward that area to check for a hot cow and size up the bugling bull to see if he can be challenged for the right to mate the cow.

Several bulls may converge on the area, and if one or more cows is in heat, peak rut activity commences, with several bulls madly bugling their excitement and chasing other cows and competing bulls. It's a wild time in the elk woods, and a prime opportunity for a bowhunter. Unfortunately, peak rut activity is short-lived and often occurs at night or during the week when a working man is on the job. In other words, it's easy to miss the peak of the elk rut.

So why not "create" your own peak of the rut? That's exactly what I do when I use my Peak Rut Elk Calling method. By the first of September, I feel confident that most bulls are hard horned and capable of mating. In Colorado, where archery season begins the last week in August, I hike along ridges searching for elk rubs. A rubbed tree means there's a hard horned bull nearby, and a hard horned bull is a bull that can be called in and killed.

I begin peak rut elk calling by choosing an area that affords good ambush cover. I then begin bugling loudly, throwing cow calls back and forth, then more short grunts, squeaky bugles, and long drawn-out bugles. I've been told by embarrassed bowhunters who were drawn in by my peak rut elk calling that it even got them excited because it sounded like a whole herd of elk had erupted.

One or more bulls may begin bugling back, their intensity and frequency increasing with their excitement. Eventually, I'll notice a bull coming closer to investigate, and I then look for a good ambush spot. Depending upon the actions of the bull, I may go to cow calling as I attempt to lure the bull in to bow range. If that doesn't work, I'll go back to squeaky bugling mixed with cow calls to assure the bull that I'm a

A rubbed tree means there's a hard-antlered bull nearby. Such an animal can be called in and killed.

small bull with a hot cow, thereby allaying his fear of being punished by a big nasty brute. More often than not, a bull will come forward to find out what the heck all the commotion is about.

That's the situation I found myself in the day before I met those bowhunters on the trail in Colorado. I'd hiked for about three miles along a high dividing ridge between two large drainages and set up a spike camp at the brow of the ridge. My camp consisted of a small lightweight tent and sleeping bag, plus water and provisions for a three-day stay. I'd been told about this area by a friend, who said that there were a lot of bulls on the finger ridges that ran down from the main ridge.

With camp in order, I sat on a rock in the warm late summer sun and studied the ridges below. I decided to drop off the point of the main ridge and begin traversing across each ridge and draw, peak rut elk calling as I went.

Two hours before sunset, I dropped down about a thousand feet and eased onto a small ridge. I called for several minutes without a response, so I moved across to another ridge about two hundred yards away. I found a fresh elk rub, so I knew a bull was somewhere in the area. I set up behind a tree on the downwind side of a game trail, facing toward a cool draw where the elk would be holed-up to escape the heat of the day.

After calling for five minutes with no answer, I heard a noise behind me, but I discounted it. No elk in his right mind would be out on that hot oak brush infested sidehill. Probably, I thought, just a mule deer. I finally gave up and stood, but when I looked back, I was shocked to see an alert five-point bull elk staring at me fifty yards away. After the bull had crashed off into the oak brush, I shook my head and silently chastised myself with the thought, "Maybe you don't know everything there is to know about elk."

I hiked to the next ridge, which also had dense oak brush on the south-facing side, and dark spruce and aspen thickets on the cool north side. Fresh elk tracks littered the ground, and several spruce and aspen saplings had been rubbed recently. I began peak rut elk calling, throwing long and short bugles ahead and behind me, interspersed with lots of excited cow calls and mews. A few minutes into my setup, I heard a raspy chirp below the ridge to my left.

The sound didn't resemble a bull's bugle, more like a raven's croak, but I remembered a few years back when I called into a shallow draw and got only a raven to respond. But as I moved up, a six-point bull had trotted away. Since then, I'd fallen into the habit of considering any strange noise in the woods as suspicious.

Could the sound I'd just heard have come from a bull? I began peppering the draw with squeaky bugles. I'd called about a dozen times when I heard it – a low, hoarse grunt. Adrenalin shot through me, and I frantically searched for a good ambush spot, but a more pressing problem arose. The late afternoon heat was still sending a thermal breeze from the ridge top into the draw. If I was to have any chance at that bull, I'd have to get off that ridge – fast!

I ran down the crest of the ridge for a hundred yards, then eased over the side. When I got to the elevation where I guessed the bull was located, I checked the wind. It was blowing almost in my face. I dared not advance because I had no idea where the bull was, so I turned away and threw a soft, squeaky bugle. A second later, the bull replied with a low, raspy bugle from about seventy yards away.

I scooted forward fifteen yards and hid behind a thicket of small red fir trees. I turned away and bugled again. This time the bull's bugle came back crisp and loud, with an anger in it that set my hands to trembling. I nocked an arrow and slipped forward to a small, limby tree and bugled again. The bull responded immediately, and I heard the swish

The author with the big six-point bull killed on August 30th using Peak Rut Calling.

of trees and the loud pounding of hooves on the forest floor.

As I studied the area ahead, the bull's rack appeared, dark brown with ivory-colored tips, and seemed to float above the small fir trees. The bull broke into an opening about fifteen yards below me. I cow called and the bull stopped. His blazing eyes were just beginning to show fear when the two-blade Magnus broadhead sliced through his chest. The bull galloped into an aspen thicket below. I listened intently, heard a loud cough, followed by another, then a loud crash. The bull was dead when I got to him. He was a magnificent animal with a large sweeping six-point rack that later scored just above the Pope & Young record book minimum.

And consider this. While I was feasting my eyes on the tremendous trophy animal lying at my feet, the two bowhunters I mentioned at the beginning of this chapter were probably giving up on their hunt in disgust, vowing to not return to the elk woods until the rut started. Hmm!

Since the date was August 30th, my guess is that my bull had not yet begun bugling, and my peak rut calling had prompted him to rasp out his first feeble bugle, though his last had sounded pretty good. In further examining this hunt, I want to point out that Peak Rut Elk Calling has the philosophy of aggressive elk hunting at its roots. If I hadn't aggressively moved from ridge to ridge, hadn't aggressively called, hadn't aggressively confronted that bull, I would have gone home as discouraged and empty handed as those two bowhunters I met later while blissfully struggling under a load of elk meat.

How to Peak Rut Elk Call

There are two key elements to Peak Rut Elk Calling. First, never forget that you're trying to simulate the frenzied calling of an elk herd in the peak of the rut. You have to shrug off the tendency to be tentative. You have to call a lot. It's not unusual for me to bugle a half dozen times in one minute, with cow calls in between. I'll keep that up for about five minutes, and then I'll wait another few minutes just in case a bull comes in silently like that five-point Colorado bull who slipped in behind me. This is a common problem early in September when some bulls have not yet begun bugling regularly.

You'll eventually encounter a few bowhunters who think you're nuts to be doing so much calling, and they'll surely mention that you're over-calling and chasing the bulls away. If that happens, just ask them, "And how many bulls have you brought in with your wimpy calling?"

But if no elk respond, don't sit on a ridge for an hour wearing out your bugle. If an elk is in the area and interested, you'll hear from him within a few minutes. If you haven't seen or heard anything, move on to another area. In the early season, I've noticed that I sometimes have to move in closer to an area where I know bulls are lurking before they respond.

Second, you should remember that the Peak Rut Calling method is the process by which you fool a nearby bull into thinking a hot cow is in the area. Once you get him interested and moving in, you should tone down your brisk bugling pace, or you run the risk of intimidating him. I usually wait to see if the incoming bull responds better to a bugle or a cow call. That's what I did with that big Colorado bull. He ignored my repeated cow calls, but responded to my bugling, so I guessed he was the dominant bull in that drainage who took exception to some lesser bull moving in on his cows.

Several times I've killed wary bulls that responded to my Peak Rut Elk Calling, by switching to cow calls. But if a bull's responses lose

When Peak Rut Elk Calling, it is important to remember that you are trying to simulate the frenzied calling of an elk herd in the peak of the rut. That means lots of bugling and cow calls.

their fire, I'll start bugling at him again to see if that's what gets him excited.

But during the excitement of the encounter, it is sometimes dangerous to start thinking too much about what a bull is thinking. It's wise to remember that an elk is an animal prone to instinctive urges. His response may be without any discernable (at least to a human) rhyme or reason, so you've got to arm yourself with an arsenal of calling and hunting methods, and then find the one that trips a bull's trigger. Remember, the object of the hunt is to get a bull into bow range and kill him. How this is accomplished depends greatly on a bull's reactions to what you throw at him. Twice, I've brought in hesitant bulls by finally clamming up and simply mimicking the soft grunts they were emitting.

In conclusion, Peak Rut Elk Calling is a briskly paced hunting method capable of getting the bulls interested and excited anytime during the rut, thereby opening the window to a plethora of other new calls and tactics that the bull has probably not been exposed to. It's then just a simple chore to use a new ruse or gimmick to get him into bow range.

Mike's first set of rattling antlers came from a forked-horn bull. They worked well, but proved to be too unwieldy.

Chapter 4

NEW AND EXPERIMENTAL
ELK HUNTING CALLS AND METHODS

A few years ago I was asked by Bow Masters Magazine to host a sportsman who had won a free elk bowhunt. It sounded like fun, so I agreed. I also realized it would be a challenge because our hunt was planned for an area of northwestern Colorado that saw intense hunting pressure every September from an army of bowhunters who bombarded the elk with every call on the market.

I decided to arrive a few days early and hopefully kill a bull so I could concentrate on helping the prize winner, Paul Headley of New Jersey, get an elk. It took me just two days to kill a nice five-point bull, and that left me with a couple days to hang out before Paul arrived. I took this opportunity to work on some new and experimental elk hunting tactics.

My first opportunity arrived shortly after dawn when I encountered a bull bugling from a large stand of dark timber below a ridge. I moved in and tried every call I could think of, but the bull wouldn't come in, and it became obvious that he'd heard it all before. He refused to budge from his timbered thicket, so I decided to try a new hunting technique that I'd been experimenting with.

I quit calling and pulled a plastic deer rattling box from my pocket. Most bowhunters would have thought I was nuts to be in the elk woods making loud grinding and clacking sounds, but there was a method to my madness, and from the reaction I was getting from the bull just ahead, it was working.

As I clacked loudly with the rattle box, the bull's bugling intensified. He moved closer and began raking his antlers on a spruce sapling about sixty yards away. I worked the rattling box again, and the bull broke out of the thicket, heading straight at me. He stopped about fifteen yards away, ignored me hunkered down behind a tree, and surveyed the forest for the two bulls he'd heard fighting. Finally, he sniffed the air and bolted. As I watched that fine animal trot off, I couldn't resist a gloating snicker, because I'd proven once again that new elk calling methods will fool hard-hunted elk.

I am happy to report that the science of elk hunting is still evolving. (Or should I say adapting!) Elk are quick learners. Those calls and methods that once worked so well become overused and eventually educate the elk, so something new is needed that the elk have not wised up to.

The good news is that new calls and hunting methods have shown great promise in attracting over-hunted, call-shy bulls. Some of these methods were considered foolish gimmicks a few years ago, but are now an important part of an experienced bowhunter's bag of tricks.

Specifically, I've been experimenting with rattling, glunking and decoying, plus a different type of hot cow call, and some calling modifications with the standard hot cow call. After I finished hosting the Colorado bowhunt (Paul Headley missed two shots at elk in five days), I returned to my home in Montana and decided to not shoot a second bull that fall. Instead, I dedicated the rest of my Montana archery season to testing some of these new techniques in an atmosphere where I could sit back and try some wild and crazy stuff without feeling frustrated if I didn't kill a bull.

Rattling

I became interested in rattling for elk by accident a few years ago while photographing a huge herd bull near Banff, Alberta. By staying safely back about eighty yards and using a 600 millimeter telephoto lens, I'd been rewarded with many great photos of this bull until the sun warmed the land and the herd bedded in a thicket. I was about to leave when I heard the clack of antlers in the forest a hundred yards away. I slipped forward and discovered two large five-point bulls in a friendly pushing match.

While my camera whirred, the herd bull began bugling furiously. The clacking antlers had fired him up, and a minute later the enraged bull left his harem of cows and stomped toward the smaller satellite bulls, who scattered when the big guy arrived.

I thought, "Hmm! Was this an isolated incident, or did the clack of antlers in the elk woods trip a rut-crazed bull elk's emotional trigger?" Calling or luring elk is illegal in a national park or preserve, so I couldn't pursue the idea at the time, but I did make a note in my "to do" list to experiment with this technique.

Of course, the notion of rattling for elk raises an immediate logistical problem. A mature bull elk's antlers are four feet long and weigh up to thirty pounds. No way was I going to pack a set of those things around in the elk woods all day!

I settled for a pair of forked antlers from a yearling bull, which I brought along on an elk photography trip to Colorado. One morning, I spotted two young bulls pushing at each other, while a larger bull bugled at them seventy yards away. I hid behind a large rock about 150 yards from the sparring bulls and began loudly clacking and grinding the forked horn antlers. After a few minutes of working the antlers, I raised up to see what effect it had on the elk. All three elk were standing there within bow range, seeking the phantom bulls who were sparring.

A week later I used the same antlers while guiding my friend, Ohne Rausch of Wisconsin. One morning we set up in a high country aspen grove, with Ohne hidden about forty yards in front of me. I began cow calling, then started in rattling. Within seconds, I heard hooves pounding on the forest floor above us. Two cows trotted down to us,

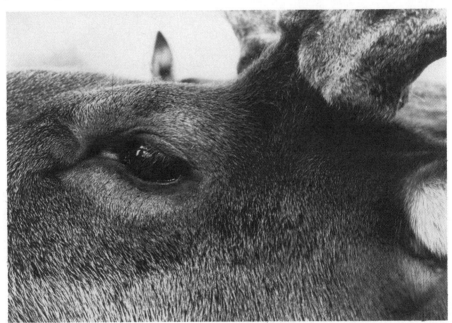

Elk are quick learners. Those calls and methods that once worked so well have been overused and eventually educated the elk, so something new is needed that the elk have not wised up to.

intensely curious about the unusual sounds in their draw. Ohne decided to pass up the cows and was rewarded a few days later with his first elk, a nice four-point bull.

But even those forked elk antlers became cumbersome after I returned to the brushy Montana forests along the Idaho border. I searched for an alternative and eventually discovered a dandy substitute. I began experimenting with a Lohman long distance deer rattling box, which consists of a hard plastic box with two heavy plastic plates inside which slide back and forth. By pressing hard against these plates, I was able to simulate the heavy grinding and clacking sounds typical of two bull elk fighting.

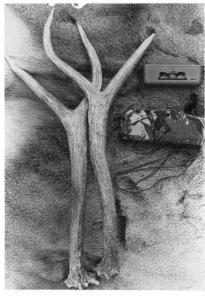

Besides real elk antlers, a heavy duty deer rattling box also worked well for rattling in bulls.

Another nice feature of the Lohman rattle box was that I could operate it with one hand, while holding my bow up and ready with the other. I also tried a deer rattling bag, which works by rubbing several plastic rods enclosed in a cotton bag, but the volume and sound was not deep enough to suit me.

During my fall of experimenting in Montana, I rattled in two bulls – a small four-point raghorn and a mature five-point bull – plus four cows. The bulls were lured in by mixing low intensity bugling with the rattling. Two cows came in when I was just rattling, and two came in when I was cow calling and rattling.

I also had two negative experiences while rattling. Once, I had a small five-point bull hung up about seventy yards away. He was raking his antlers on a tree and responding to my cow calls and bugling, but he wouldn't come in. When I switched to rattling, the bull stared in my direction for a few minutes before retreating in a stiff-legged gait, finally trotting as he went out of sight. I also had two cows come in, stop at sixty yards, then trot off. In both cases, I rattled long and hard, and this overuse may have startled the elk.

As a result of my experiments, I would suggest that you try rattling early in the season, before the bulls have become vocal and are newly hard-horned. This is the period when they enjoy a friendly pushing match. During the peak of the rut, I would use conventional calling methods first, and if they don't work, then switch to rattling to lure in a hesitant bull.

Glunking

Glunking is a seldom heard sound that is made by a herd bull when he is tending his cows. It's one of the most exciting sounds you'll hear in elk country because it means you're very close to a herd bull. Unlike the loud, piercing squeal of a bugle, a bull's glunk is a soft, gluppy "glunk-glunk-glunk" sound that does not carry far. Only the herd bull makes this sound. You won't hear a lonely bachelor bull or raghorn glunking as they wander the elk woods.

I've heard this glunking sound many times while photographing herd bulls with their cows, but it's only been the past few seasons that I've begun experimenting with it. I quickly discovered that a glunking call brought almost no reaction when it was used a hundred yards away from a bull and his harem of cows. But when I moved in closer to the cows, it often created a frenzied reaction from the herd bull, who was enraged that another bull had slipped in and was tending one of his cows.

During my month of experimentation in Montana, I first followed a herd bull for almost a mile while he pushed his cows into the head of a brush-choked draw. The elk finally stopped in the brush, and I was able to move within forty yards of the herd bull in the dense cover. Though I couldn't see the bull, I caught glimpses of cows within twenty yards. I bugled and got a fierce challenging bugle from the herd bull, but he would not come closer. Then I began glunking. Twice, I emitted a series of soft, "glunk-glunk-glunks."

The bull screamed out a bugle and charged past me in the brush, but then he caught my scent and the entire herd crashed off. If that brush had not been so dense, I believe that bull would have presented a killing shot because he was no more than fifteen yards away when he went past me. Consequently, I was very pleased with my first glunking experiment.

Glunking is a sound seldom heard in the elk woods. It's made by a herd bull tending his cows. This Rake & Brake elk bugle produces a passable glunk by tapping the mouthpiece with the palm of the hand.

However, I was disappointed with my next encounter because the herd bull did not come toward me when I began glunking about thirty yards away from his cows. This smallish five-point bull continued bugling, even raked his antlers on a tree, but would not come closer. It's hard to guess if the bull might have eventually come in, because the hunt ended abruptly when a curious cow walked right up to me and stuck her nose through the bush I was hiding behind. She barked out a warning and the whole herd thundered off.

I also tried glunking at a few satellite bulls, but received little or no notice. In my opinion, the jury is still out on glunking as a calling method. However, I do believe it to be a valid method of bringing in a herd bull if you can slip in close to his cows.

There are a few commercial glunking calls on the market, but the best I've found is Lohman's Rake & Brake elk bugle. To make a passable glunk, you just pop the mouthpiece with the palm of your hand, and the wide bell at the other end amplifies the sound. The nice thing about the Rake & Brake call is that it's primarily a grunt tube to be used to amplify a mouth diaphragm, and having a glunking capability furnishes you with a free call for your arsenal without having to wrap another lanyard and call around your neck.

Decoying

Decoying has been around for several years, but has not caught on with elk bowhunters, mostly because the first commercial elk decoys were large and noisy and difficult to pack around in the elk woods. However, in the past two years I've found a few cow elk decoys that are lightweight, quiet and easy to set up.

My Montana experiments with cow elk decoys occurred in open lodgepole forest. First, I used a Featherflex decoy which, strangely, has no head. This foam rubber roll-up decoy is suspended between two trees with elastic bungy cords. It is quick and easy to set up if there are two trees handy, but it can't be used in open country, where a decoy is needed the most.

Another decoy that I used and liked a lot is the Montana Brand cow decoy. It is carried as a fourteen-inch diameter flat pack, and springs open to almost the full size of a cow elk. Thin metal rods are shoved into the ground to keep this decoy upright, so it can be used in the forests of the Northern Rockies, or the open sage and bull pine flats of the Southwest.

My first decoying success occurred on a knife ridge across from the head of a draw where a bull had bugled. I set up a Featherflex decoy in a small opening, then hid twenty yards away behind a small bush on the downwind side. I began cow calling, and a five-point bull came out of the draw and walked within fifteen yards of me. He stopped twenty yards from the decoy, eyed it suspiciously, then spotted me and trotted off.

I had a bit more success with the Montana Brand decoy, probably because I began using it more. It was less bulky and just as quick to set up. Oh yes, it also has a head. One time, I set this decoy up on an open sidehill and hastily hid behind a skinny lodgepole pine tree a second before a five-point bull appeared. That bull walked right up to the decoy, posturing as it came, but when it got fifteen yards away, it became alert, finally extending it's head and scrutinizing the decoy. Then it turned and walked away in a stiff-legged gait.

Though the decoy worked, this encounter also showed me that it's not a good idea to wait in ambush right next to the decoy. An approaching elk is prone to became suspicious when it got to the twenty yard range of a decoy. For that reason, it's best to set up your decoy, then move out in front of it about thirty-five yards and set up an ambush before the bull gets too close to the decoy.

Another perplexing problem that I observed is that a decoy will occasionally spook a younger bull. Twice, I've had two-year-old bulls spot the decoy, stare at it for a few minutes, then trot away. One time when I was bowhunting in Colorado with my friend, Dennis Williams, we encountered a bugling bull, and Dennis quickly set up a decoy, then began cow calling. I hid about thirty yards in front, and off to the side of the decoy.

The bull bugled twice and came in at a trot, but when it spotted the decoy, it skidded to a halt and stood broadside to me at forty yards, staring intently at the decoy. I didn't feel comfortable attempting a shot that far with my recurve bow, so I watched as the bull paced back and forth for five minutes while staring suspiciously at the decoy about fifty

Rex Rogers of Colstrip, Montana, says, "This Montana Brand decoy is the answer I was looking for to bugle in bulls and get a good shot when hunting by myself. This bull stopped at 15 yards and bugled, then came right on by at 10 yards headed for the decoy. I've had people look at the picture and not realize that one of those elk is a decoy. Obviously, the bull was fooled also."

yards away. The bull finally spotted me and trotted off. I have no explanation why a young bull might become tentative when he sees a decoy. To counter that, I've also had a few raghorn bulls come right in to my decoy.

Setting up a decoy and calling an elk into range can be hectic for a single hunter. For that reason, I believe a decoy works best for guys who like to double-team elk. The caller can set up the decoy and begin calling from behind it, while the shooter hurries forward to set up an ambush without worrying about calling or the decoy's position.

Of course, this would be no problem if you were hunting alone from a blind or over a wallow or water hole, where a decoy would be a great lure to bring a suspicious bull those last few yards into bow range. Montana resident Joe Egan was hunting in the early season along a series of marshy water holes. The problem was that the elk might come in just about anywhere to drink, so Joe set up a Montana Brand cow elk decoy about twenty yards from his ground blind. A half hour later, a five-point bull came down the trail. The bull spotted the cow decoy and started for it, allowing Joe to draw back and make a perfect chest shot. The bull bolted, but when Joe cow-called, the bull stopped and stared at the decoy again. Then it stumbled and dropped.

Hot Cow Calls

The hot cow call is a good example of the adaptability of the elk. Just a few years ago it was the rage among elk archery hunters. Its high pitched, nasal twang seemed to lure in those bulls who ignored bugling, and for a few years we bowhunters experienced staggering success. On one Colorado hunt, I brought a stubborn bull on the run for 400 yards after I began wailing on a hot cow call. Word about the hot cow calls spread fast – too fast. Now, just about every bowhunter carries one or more hot cow calls around his neck, and what was once a secret weapon is now being blown in excess, and the elk have wised up to it.

So should we throw away our hot cow calls? No way! I still use mine to bring in elk, but I also use it judiciously because I know that a hot cow call has the potential to send a rutting bull elk either way – running to the caller, or running away! A hot cow call mimics the excited call of a cow elk. But what has her excited? Is she caught up in the peak of the rut, anxiously calling out as she comes into heat, or is she anxious because she is suspicious of danger?

That's the quandary that a bull elk is presented with when you start wailing on a hot cow call. Is the excited cow just out of sight calling

Hot cow calls mimic the excited call of a cow elk. But is the cow rut excited, or scared excited? Call too much on a hot cow call, and you may scare off a bull. It's best to get a bull interested first with bugles and common cow calls before turning to a hot cow call.

because she is sexually excited, or is she scared excited? Wail too much, and you may send the wrong message to that bull and chase him away. I don't have enough fingers and toes to count the times bowhunters have related to me in disgust how they had a bull interested, but he trotted off when they switched to a hot cow call.

For that reason, many experienced elk hunters don't use a hot cow call anymore. They rely instead on basic cow calls that don't carry the high, excited pitch that has the potential to make or break a promising hunt.

I firmly believe that the hot cow call has a place around the neck of every bowhunter. But you can't go afield with the idea that you can use it like the Pied Piper, blissfully drawing in every bull elk in the woods, and you can't hide behind a tree and start wailing on a hot cow call and expect results. You'll end up chasing away more elk than you bring in.

I use my hot cow call a lot when I Peak Rut Elk Call. Besides bugling and cow calling, I'll add a few hot cow calls because I want to throw in all the elk sounds that a herd in the frenzy of the rut will use. If

I get a bull interested, and he has advanced toward me, I'll sometimes try a hot cow call. Remember, the bull is already aware that there are bulls and cows up ahead, so he's not prone to become wary when he hears an excited cow call. He actually expects the loud, plaintive bleat of an impatient cow, and it's exactly this effect that a hot cow call is made for. It draws in that interested bull those extra few yards to get a piece of that "hot" cow who's doing all the "excited" calling.

My good friend, Paul Brown, is a master elk caller and expert hunting guide. Paul often uses his hot cow calls to culminate an elk encounter. A few years ago, he was guiding outdoor writer John Sloan while we were working on an elk hunting video. Paul located a distant bull, and both men hurried forward until Paul eased into a red fir-aspen hillside and whispered for John to slip forward and set up about fifty yards ahead. Paul bugled, and the bull bugled back from about 200 yards. Paul then began cow calling, and the bull moved closer, but still didn't come in. Paul then began wailing on a Wayne Carlton "Fightin' Cow Call." That bull bugled furiously and came in at a trot, panting in lust. John shot the bull as it passed by at twenty yards. You can see this amazing hunting sequence in the video, *"Double Teaming Bulls."* It is a classic example of the proper use of a hot cow call.

Mew Calls

Some experienced elk hunters feel so strongly that the hot cow calls often send a tone of danger instead of excitement, that they have sought an alternative call that still attracts the bulls. Ralph Meline of Abe & Son Natural Elk Sounds is such a person. Ralph told me, "I never did like the hot cow calls. Way too much high tone. It's not a natural sound in a calm elk woods. It scares some bulls."

So Ralph designed a series of estrus cow calls, culminating in his latest invention, the 63M Molestus Estrus Cow Call. This call lacks the hysterical high pitch of the hot cow calls, relying instead on a strong nasal tone. These distinctive mews accomplish the same "pleading" tone as the hot cow call, with little danger of alerting an incoming bull.

The new mew cow calls tend to become lost among the pile of hot cow calls currently flooding the market, so I doubt they will have the huge impact like the hot cow calls had their first few years. But these mew cow calls have the potential to become just as valuable to an elk hunter because of their more natural pleading sound and lower nasal tone.

New Calls on the Market

(Author's note: I am not financially tied to any of the following companies, and will not receive any financial gain from mentioning a product. My intention is to simply help my fellow bowhunters find new and exciting elk calls that work.)

There are some new elk calls available at your sporting goods store or outdoor catalog that you may want to check out. Though there are many new calls out there, I'll only mention the ones that I've personally tried and like. Others may be just as good, but I haven't gotten around to trying them.

Primos has come out with a unique hand-held cow call, the Hoochie Mama, which uses a soft rubber air bellows that you push in with your thumb. This call has three settings, but I particularly liked the "mew" setting because of its more mellow, nasal tone. This call can be used by itself, or in conjunction with a mouth diaphragm to create a peak rut effect of a lot of excited cows calling at once.

As I mentioned, Abe & Son's Molestus Estrus cow call is an excellent alternative to using a hot cow call. It's distinctive, nasal mew tone is loud enough to be heard at a distance, but not so shrill as to spook

Ralph Meline's big bull is proof that the lower tone of a Mew Call is less likely to spook an incoming elk.

an incoming elk.

Lohman's Rake & Brake elk bugle deserves attention because it is so versatile. It not only acts as a grunt tube to amplify a mouth bugling diaphragm, but by popping the mouthpiece end with the palm of your hand, you can make decent glunking sounds. However, the best feature of the Rake & Brake elk call, in my opinion, is the thin bellows at the end, which was designed to be rubbed against a tree to simulate a bull raking his antlers.

Many archers don't know how hard to rake a tree in response to a bull's raking, or a tree limb is not handy when needed, and they don't want to move around too much. The loud grinding/raking sound this call makes by simply twisting the thin corrugated plastic bellows against a tree trunk is impressive.

In conclusion, we have at our disposal a number of new and experimental elk hunting calls and techniques to help us face the adapting elk herd of today. And by the time the elk get wise to these "new" techniques, we'll have "newer" calls and techniques to stay one step ahead of those hard-hunted, call-shy bulls. Sounds like fun, doesn't it?

A bull elk may weigh upwards to a half ton. Adequate archery gear is necessary to insure a quick, humane kill.

Chapter 5

WASTED OPPORTUNITIES
MISTAKES THAT DOOM A HUNT

I have listened to hundreds of bowhunters' tales of missed opportunities, those botched hunts that we sit back later and think about and realize that we had a golden opportunity to kill a big bull, but allowed a silly mistake to doom the hunt. Following are some of the most obvious mistakes that I've seen or heard bowhunters make. Most could have easily been avoided beforehand, while others required just a little in-field adjustment. Consequently, this chapter is separated into a "Before the Hunt" and "During the Hunt" section.

–BEFORE THE HUNT–
Improper Archery Equipment

Improper archery equipment is responsible for the vast majority of botched elk hunts. Nonresidents are especially prone to arriving out West for their dream elk hunt woefully equipped to kill a bull. Many archers bring bows that are too light to handle the heavy muscled, big boned elk's anatomy, and their arrows are too light and tipped with broadheads that fail to penetrate deep enough to kill a big bull.

Much of this equipment mess stems from archery manufacturers who make extravagant claims of success using their bows or arrows or broadheads which may be better suited for thin-skinned deer or bear. Also responsible are the archery magazines that allow articles by writers who have maybe killed one or two elk, then write an article on the subject from the standpoint of an expert. It curls my toes to pick up a magazine and spot an article titled, "Hunt Elk Like Turkeys." Elk are not turkeys. A big tom weighs about 25 pounds; a big bull weighs a half ton. Tom turkeys are exciting to hunt, but they don't make the ground shake when they come thundering forward.

My ire at this problem is directed at both the high-tech crowd and the traditional archers. Both blissfully tromp through the elk woods carrying inadequate equipment. The result is, at best, a missed opportunity. At worst, it's a wounded animal and some irresponsible archer quipping, "Oops! Oh well, that didn't work." This is the opportunity to correct your equipment shortcomings so that, no matter what goes wrong on your next elk hunt, it won't be a silly archery gear problem that could have easily been avoided long before the hunt.

The High-Tech Illusion

High-tech archery has become mired in the illusion of accuracy. On the range, compound shooters deliver pinpoint accuracy all the way out to forty yards, and I've recently read a magazine article touting fifty and sixty yard shots. I even know one wingnut who brags about his ability to make 100 yard shots. Maybe all this is true at the target range, but bullseye shooting has absolutely nothing to do with hunting. And

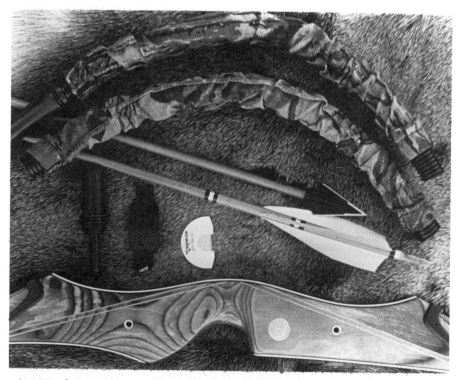

A critical part of any serious elk bowhunter's gear should be cutting edge broadheads, like this Magnus two-blade, the author's favorite elk head.

forget the ruse of 3-D shooting. Just because you're shooting at a deer or elk target, instead of a bullseye, the artificial target range conditions make whatever you're shooting at a moot point.

Under hunting conditions, an erect stance is not always possible, and a mechanical release aid that requires eight seconds to deliver an arrow is near impossible to attain. The experienced compound shooters that I hunt with have adapted their equipment and shooting style (kneeling to lower their profile) to prepare for the hunt. Most use a shooting glove or finger tab because they have more control over the bow, and they can shoot faster. Heck, even Chuck Adams avoids the complications of a mechanical release and uses a finger tab.

A few years ago, I arrived at an outfitter friend's hunting camp a day early and met a man who was on his first elk hunt. He was very excited to meet me and made a big show of asking me for pointers. So we went out to a target range where the outfitter had a full size elk target. The guy used a mechanical release, and it took him a full eight seconds at full draw to release. His arrows resembled soda straws, tipped with expandable blade broadheads.

He never got closer than thirty yards to the target and often shot back at sixty yards. I informed him that most elk were bow-killed at 20 yards or less, and that just about everything he was using and doing was detrimental to his getting an elk. I explained that a four-inch group at forty yards was unnecessary with an animal as big as an elk, with a killing zone roughly sixteen inches high and eighteen inches long. I also suggested that he use a finger tab instead of the mechanical release. After pestering me for the secrets to my success killing elk, the guy blew me off! He said he liked his equipment just the way it was and didn't intend to change a thing.

Three days later, this man's guide brought a large five-point bull in to fourteen yards, and he shot it far back, near the rump. That's a miss of about five feet! The next day, the guy gut shot a four-point bull at about eight yards, a miss of about four feet – at eight yards! The guy got back to camp, packed up, and left.

Another big problem that many compound shooters have is inefficient broadheads. A bull elk presents extreme penetrating problems for multi-blade heads. I've seen too many expandable (which expend up to 30 percent of the arrow's energy just opening) and multiple blade heads hit an elk's shoulder blade and lodge there. Some outfitters won't even allow their clients to use them on elk.

I use a Magnus two-blade broadhead, and this head has sliced right through the shoulder blade of many elk. In response to the requests of many compound shooters who are shrewdly opting for two-blade broadheads that fly true when hunting larger game, Magnus and other broadhead manufacturers offer two blade screw-in broadheads in 100 grains and 125 grains.

Poor Traditional Choices

When I first laid eyes on the hunter sneaking along a forest trail in Montana's Anaconda-Pintlar Wilderness Area, I wondered if I might have gone back in time a hundred years. The guy was dressed like an Indian and carried a crude bow. Nocked to the sinew bowstring was a homemade arrow tipped with an obsidian broadhead. While the bull elk bugled around us, a rather tense conversation took place, during which I explained in no uncertain terms that such equipment was more likely to maim an elk, than kill one.

The man, a first-time nonresident elk hunter, grudgingly accepted one of my cedar arrows tipped with a razor sharp Magnus two-blade broadhead. I never saw the guy again, but I feel confident that if he encountered an elk, he'd at least have a chance to kill it if he used my

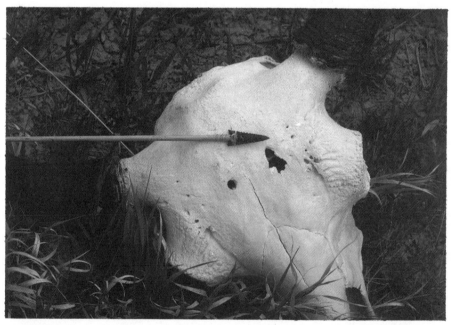

Traditional archery gear, such as this obsidian replica of an ancient Indian arrowhead, should be left at home by the elk hunter who uses traditional equipment.

arrow.

I've extensively researched Native American hunting practices with bow and arrow, and I've discovered that few elk were killed with stone heads because most Indian bows did not possess the long range (twenty yards) capability of driving a crude stone head deep into an elk's chest. Instead, Indians used snares and pits, and also drove elk into brush corrals where they were speared and peppered with arrows at close range.

I admire those hearty men who ply the historic trade of homemade bow and arrow making. Their rustic equipment is efficient enough to even kill deer, but such equipment should be left above the hearth when they go elk hunting. It just isn't powerful enough.

Traditional archers also use bows that are too light for elk hunting. Unable to pull back a sixty pound bow, many traditionalists talk themselves into believing that a fifty or fifty-five pound pull recurve will get the job done. In my opinion, it won't. Every year I hear about a few elk that have been killed with fifty-five pound recurves. Yes, if the arrow hits between a rib, a fifty-five pound pull bow has the penetrating power to kill a bull. But if anything goes wrong, such as a shoulder blade hit (sometimes even a rib will impede penetration), the lighter weight bow does not deliver the necessary kinetic energy to drive the broadhead deep into an elk's chest.

If you shoot a recurve or longbow, and you can't muster the strength to pull back and accurately shoot a bow in the sixty pound pull range, you should consider switching to a compound bow. The mechanical advantage will furnish the extra kinetic energy needed to drive your arrow into a bull's chest. I realize that this might stick in the craw of some traditional archers, but you don't have to go ultra high tech to enjoy elk hunting. Several of my friends have been forced by age-related shoulder problems to switch to a compound bow. They shoot their arrows from a flipper rest instinctively, and they've experienced no drop-off in enjoyment during the hunt.

Whether you're a high-tech or traditional archer, make sure your bow has a minimum sixty-pound pull (recurve or compound), and please consider using a two-blade broadhead, which you can easily sharpen with a hand sharper (Accusharp, etc.).

Hunting Where There Are No Elk

Hunting where there are no elk is probably the number one reason why bowhunters return from the hunt empty handed. And surprisingly, this problem not only affects the nonresident who lives far from elk

The best way to locate elk in the vast western landscape is to get on a high ridge in early morning or evening and glass and bugle into distant basins. If there's a rutting bull within hearing range, you'll soon get his response.

country, but it also plagues many archers who live just a few hours from prime elk habitat. Consider this: You can carry the best archery outfit, the hottest calls, plus a cerebral encyclopedia on elk hunting tactics – but if there aren't any elk where you're hunting, you're wasting your time.

I am dumbfounded every year to meet archers who have spent days, even weeks, roaming mile after mile of habitat that doesn't harbor elk. Often times, the problem is that these archers are hunting too low, in those mid-elevation zones where the elk lived in early summer while they waited for the deep snows to melt up high. These areas will still show some sign of elk – droppings, tracks, trails, etc.– but the elk have left this lower country for the lush grasses in the cooler high country.

Generally, look for elk in the mountains just below timberline, where subalpine timber and secluded meadows offer food and shelter, commonly referred to as prime elk habitat. But even in these places, elk are not found everywhere. The western landscape is just too big, and the elk too scattered.

The best way to find out if elk live in the area you're hunting is to get on a high ridge and glass the openings in early morning or late evening, or hike the crest of a high ridge and bugle into basins and ridges

One of the overlooked tragedies that I encounter every fall is a hunter who has done his homework – found a good elk area, gotten into good physical condition – only to have his footwear fail him. A few blisters can ruin an entire elk hunt.

still needs to be in good shape because the elk travel long distances in the Southwest – often five miles from bed to feed and another five miles from feed to water. More than once, I've had to give up because I got tuckered out while chasing elk in those "easy" rolling hills in New Mexico.

In other words, short of hunting on a game farm, you're going to have to be in decent physical condition if you expect to score on an elk. You can hike, bike, run – whatever – just so you get your cardiovascular system revved up. My friend, Jim Kingsley, works at a huge General Motors Plant in Janesville, Wisconsin. Jim told me that a small army of men and women at the plant who are planning fall hunts converge on the stairwells during lunch hour and walk or run up hundreds of stairs. Jim said the stairways have become an informal source of hunting news and a great place to glean information about where the good elk hunting areas can be found in a distant state.

One of the overlooked tragedies that I encounter every fall is a hunter who has done his homework – found the elk, gotten in good shape – only to have his footwear fail him. Last fall in western Montana I met a man from Michigan who had such badly blistered feet that he could barely walk and was planning to go home after just three days. He told me, "I got in good shape, and I even worked out with my hunting boots on, figuring that would toughen my feet. But the steep side hills made my feet roll inside my boots. After a hard hike the first day, the bottoms of my feet were sore. I hunted hard in the rain the next morning, and my feet got wet and blistered. Now, I can't hardly even walk. It'll take a couple weeks to heal the soles of my feet. I might as well go home."

Everyone is prone to blisters (including me), if you overwork your feet on rough ground. Heck, I was with a guy whose feet were a mass of blisters after walking just four miles in gently rolling hills in eastern Montana last fall. While it's a good idea to toughen your feet as much as possible and break in new hunting boots beforehand, blisters happen. The key is to avoid them as much as possible and carry first aid that can nip the problem before it become a mass of raw skin that covers virtually the entire sole of your foot.

I wear lightweight uninsulated Gortex-lined Danner boots. Forget the insulation for archery hunting. It's warm, often too warm. You want lightweight and comfort on your feet because the nature of elk hunting requires long distance hiking over uneven terrain.

But sooner or later, it'll happen – that sore spot on the bottom of your foot. I always carry a few narrow and wide band aids. Slap a band-aid on a small blister forming on your heel, and the problem disappears. It's that simple. For the soles of my feet, I carry moleskin. This stuff is a life saver.

And if my feet get sore, I'll wear light hiking shoes or high-arched athletic shoes when conditions allow, such as an afternoon hunt when it's dry and warm. My friend, Dwight Schuh, often wears high top boat and deck shoes with Gore-tex lined socks even in wet weather. He says this combination keeps his feet dry as long as boots.

In rainy weather, I always wear uninsulated rubber boots made by La Crosse. These boots are ankle snug, designed that way to avoid the slipping and sliding of the foot inside the boot, the main cause of blisters.

– DURING THE HUNT –

Hunting Too Slow

God gave elk long legs for a good reason. Elk country is so big that elk need those long legs to roam over large areas of the vast elk woods in a short amount of time as they move from bedding areas to feed and water. A casual pace for an elk is about seven miles per hour, which is a brisk pace for a jogger. Many times, I've exhausted myself trying to catch up to an elk that was unaware I was after him, and was moving at a leisurely pace.

If all that wasn't bad enough, the elk accomplish their feed to bed routine in about two hours after first light. And once an elk tunnels into his favorite bedding thicket, he become lethargic and largely unresponsive. A bowhunter who hunts too slow is going to miss valuable opportunities, even if he locates rutting bulls.

Hunting too slow is one of those vague problems that is easy to fall into, especially if you're primarily a deer hunter who has spent years perfecting the necessary deer hunting stealth (silence and slow movement) to get within range of a furtive whitetail. But it's different with an elk. A mature bull is big and fast-moving, and he isn't afraid of his shadow. His weight also creates a large amount of noise when he walks through the woods, so he's not alarmed when he hears another elk moving just out of sight in the woods. In other words, you can move fast and make noise around elk, and get away with it. An occasional cow call tells any unseen elk who hears you that you're just another cow moving through the area.

Elk move at a fast clip. To be successful hunting them, you must also move through the elk woods at a brisk pace.

Elk are fast learners. After a few days hunting them without success, the animals will become tentative and much more wary. It's best to move to another area for a few days and allow that riled up elk herd to settle down.

I've even brought bulls in just by making noise while walking through the woods. One time in Idaho, I arrived at the top of a high, brushy ridge before dawn and started pushing through the dense willow and alder toward a shallow draw where I'd heard a bull bugling the previous evening. A bugle ripped through the air about sixty yards off to my right, followed by the swish of oncoming antlers against brush. The bull was coming in because he'd heard me and thought I was an elk! I hurriedly backtracked, but the bull caught my scent and crashed off.

If you are a whitetail hunter, leave all your valuable deer hunting prowess at home and plan on moving briskly through the elk woods to intercept a bull before he arrives at his bedding area.

Wearing Out the Elk

Last fall, I met two Michigan bowhunters who were camped in an idyllic meadow near the Idaho border. They were excited to meet me, but a bit discouraged that they hadn't located any bugling bulls. I knew the area well, and offered to show them a few areas where I'd hunted rutting bulls in the past. The guys jumped at the opportunity and eagerly followed me along a trail that rimmed two large basins. While I pointed out several good areas in those basins, a bull bugled from a finger ridge beside a marshy draw. The men were ecstatic!

I stopped by their camp the next day and they greeted me with stories of frenzied bugling action with big bulls and near misses. I heard more of the same the next day, and the day after that. I jokingly mentioned that they were wearing the elk out, and they should maybe try some other areas for a few days to give the elk a chance to settle down. They looked at me like I was nuts. They returned to the same side hills again and again, and by the last day or their hunt, they coaxed only an occasional squeak from the call-shy bulls.

As I've mentioned in previous chapters, elk are quick learners, and you can quickly educate an elk herd after just a few hunts, during which several elk see or smell you. I call it "wearing out the elk," and it's one of those vague problem areas that unknowing bowhunters often fall victim to. They tell me, "I had these three bulls going crazy the first day, but then they cooled off and wouldn't hardly answer my calls after that. What happened?"

My usual reply is, "You probably wore them out with your bugling and all the scent you left behind."

It is difficult for a bowhunter, myself included, to walk away from an area where elk are rutting, but there comes a time when you have to admit that your presence has made the herd wary. When it happens to me, I leave that educated elk herd alone, give them time to settle down and return to their previous routine. I might try a neighboring drainage for a day or two, and if I don't find rutting elk there, I then return to my original hotspot. Often times, the elk have lost their wariness during my absence.

Hunting Too Close To Camp

You may find good elk hunting close to your camp during those first few days of the hunt, but after "Wearing Out The Elk", you'd be wise to find another place to hunt. But many bowhunters are hesitant to penetrate the wilderness farther than a mile, which is where the best elk hunting starts. Most areas close to access roads harbor elk, but they've been educated by lots of other hunters besides yourself, and the bulls tend to be younger animals. The farther back you go from access roads, the less wary and educated the bulls will be, and you'll experience awesome hunting under natural herd conditions.

To do this, you must plan to stay in the back country overnight. I always carry a Siwash, a french word used by French-Canadian trappers

A Siwash (overnight camp) is a favorite of mine because it allows me to stay close to the elk without wearing myself out hiking back and forth to camp.

of yesteryear which means an overnight stay in the woods. Sometimes, I'll carry a small roll up tent (about two pounds), or my Siwash may be just a space blanket to keep the dew off me during the night. Add grub and water, and that's enough to sustain me for a day or two.

Siwash is a favorite of mine for two reasons. It gets me away from other hunters close to roads, and I can hunt in the evening without worrying about the dark. Even though elk hunting is excellent in the evening (almost half my forty bow-killed elk were taken in the evening), I firmly believe that most hunters avoid serious evening hunting because they are afraid of the dark. They don't venture far from their parked vehicle or camp in the evening, for fear of falling prey to those hysterical primeval urges to rush back to the cave before the saber toothed tigers get them.

Don't laugh! I used to get that same spooky feeling at sundown, but I've solved this problem by carrying bear spray for self defense. This highly concentrated pepper spray is powerful enough to stop any saber toothed tiger my fantasies dream up. It'll also stop any lion or bear. Now, I fear nothing in the dark, even in grizzly country (though I'm very careful). As a result, I'm prone to hunt just as long and hard in the evening, and when dusk descends upon the back country, I spend a cozy night Siwashed under a tree, listening to the bulls bugle at night. At dawn I'm rested, and I know exactly where the rutting bulls are located.

I do want to mention that Siwash hunting, in my opinion, is not advisable when rain or snow descends upon the elk woods. Wet boots can lead to blistered feet; soaked clothes can lead to hypothermia. Even if you escape all that, huddling in a miserable Siwash can drain your enthusiasm. During inclement weather, it's best to retreat to your main camp and wait out the storm before penetrating the depths of the elk woods.

The upcoming chapters are loaded with solutions to specific problems that a bowhunter will encounter with rutting bull elk. As you will see, we sometimes have no control over what a rut crazed bull does in response to our bugling, and we are subject to the whims of chance, such as an errant breeze. That's the hectic, tentative nature of elk hunting. But to waste an elk hunting opportunity through poor planning or equipment choice – mistakes that could easily have been corrected before the hunt – is foolish.

Occasionally, a novice bowhunter will get lucky and encounter a bull that will come right in to his calling, but the fact remains that about 90% of the elk are being harvested by about 10% of bowhunters who have taken their elk hunting skills to a higher plane.

Chapter 6

ADVANCED ELK HUNTING

On the second day of Montana's archery season a few years back, I passed a small camp and noticed two young bowhunters standing next to a campfire. I enjoy meeting fellow bowhunters and sharing elk stories, so I pulled in to say hello. I immediately noticed an elk head with large six-point antlers in the back of a pickup.

Both men met me with a grin. "Hey!" the shorter guy exclaimed. "It's the Radical Man!"

They introduced themselves as Joe and Vern. They were first-year elk hunters, they explained, and had bought my book, *Radical Elk Hunting Strategies*. Armed with this knowledge, they had wandered into the woods the first day and bugled.

"We never called elk before," Joe said. "We bought one of those calls with the reed in it that you just blow in. We didn't even know if we were doing it right. When we got an answer from a ridge about two hundred yards away, we thought it was another hunter. We started walking away, and then I heard a noise behind us. When I looked back, I almost fainted. There's this big bull coming at us."

Vern said, "We were both in shock. We just stood there in the open. The bull walked right up to us before he finally saw us." He jabbed a finger at his partner and added, "Joe was in front so he took the first shot, but the arrow went a foot over the bull's back."

Joe grinned sheepishly and commented, "You might say I was a tad bit excited."

Vern interjected, "Then I shot and missed low."

Joe broke out in a big grin and gushed, "Then I nailed him good. He went down before he went out of sight."

"We sure are glad we read your book," Vern announced. "This bowhunting for elk is the way to go. I can't wait to get back out there tomorrow and get my elk."

Vern went back to the same ridge the next day, but didn't get his elk. He didn't get his elk the day after that, nor did he get one that season, and neither man got an elk the next season, nor the next. I kept in touch with those two young men through an archery club, and they couldn't understand what happened after such a glorious beginning.

What happened is they got lucky. They stumbled upon a bull elk in the right place at the right time, and though they gave the elk plenty of opportunity to escape with those first two missed shots, the dumb bull just stood there and let himself get killed.

The above anecdote is the exception, rather than the rule for the bowhunter. Sure, there will be an occasional easy kill when it seems like a bull is virtually committing suicide, but most experience bowhunters will tell you that for every bull who comes waltzing in to a call, there are a dozen who slip in silently, or hang up, or retreat, and it takes more than a vague notion of which end of an elk bugle to blow in to lure these bulls into bow range.

I asked Bob Robb, editor of Bow Master Magazine and an experienced elk hunter, if the bulls were getting easier for him to bring in. "Heck no!" Bob exclaimed. "I think they're getting harder. Oh, I still get an occasional easy kill when a bull comes charging in to my first call, but with most of my elk, there's always some complication that I have to deal will. I've had to resort to some wild spur-of-the-moment tactics out of desperation.

"One time," Bob mentioned, " I was closing in on a bull that had been giving me the slip. He'd hang up until I got close, then move off. As I was moving up on the bull for about the tenth time, I saw a shed elk antler lying on the ground. I'm a sucker for elk sheds, so I picked it up and dragged it along. The bull was raking his antlers on a tree about sixty yards away, so I bugled and banged a tree with the antler. I peeked above the small tree I was hiding behind and saw the bull staring in my direction. I glanced down at that shed antler and thought, 'Hmm, I wonder...'

"So I stuck the antler above the tree and waved it around. That bull bugled and came right in. I got a good shot and killed him. Who would have thought a shed antler would bring in a bull like that? Sometimes, you just have to be willing to try something new to get a bull to come in."

My most enjoyable moments hunting elk occur when I encounter that shrewd, secretive, call-shy bull who seems unhuntable, until I lure him into bow range using new calls and tactics.

I wholeheartedly agree with Bob. I've interviewed hundreds of bowhunters over two decades, and my records show that only about one in twenty bulls comes trotting in to bow range without some sort of complication. Heck, anybody can kill that one bull that trots right in. It's those other nineteen bulls who don't come blithely forward that require in-field adjustments of calling techniques and innovative hunting methods.

At about the same time I encountered Joe and Vern, the two young men I mentioned at the beginning of this chapter who got lucky their first time out, I also met another young man named Jim Kingsley. The similarities between these three young men end there. While Joe and Vern have gone through a dozen years of elkless drought, Jim has grown through those years into one of the best elk bowhunters I know, quickly learning how and why a bull elk acts and reacts, and adapting his calling and hunting tactics to suit the circumstances. You won't be reading about Jim in any magazines, or see him featured in a new elk hunting video, but maybe you should. He's a perfect example of how we can, through persistence and experience, move up from novice to an advanced level of elk hunting.

It's archers like Jim Kingsley, who have moved up to the advanced level of elk hunting, who are killing elk on a consistent basis. Consider this, 90% of the elk are being harvested by 10% of the bowhunters. That means that the same small core of experienced elk bowhunters are killing the bulls over and over again. Why? Because they've taken their sport to the next level and advanced to the point where they believe they can handle anything an elk presents them with.

I still like it when a bull comes right in to my calling, but my most enjoyable moments in the elk woods occur when I encounter that shrewd, secretive, call-shy bull who seems unhuntable. Rather than give up, I've learned to improvise and try new calls and tactics. No, I don't get every bull, but I've killed my share, and it's proven to me that no bull is unhuntable. With enough knowledge and experienced any bull can be killed if you can trip his trigger, as Bob Robb did when he waved that silly elk antler at a stubborn bull. At times, that's what it takes – something wild and crazy and as unpredictable as the animal you are hunting.

In previous chapters, you've learned how to call in bulls using the Radical (aggressive) Elk Hunting Method and Peak Rut Elk Hunting, plus some new elk calls and methods. With this knowledge, your bag of tricks is full. Even if a bull doesn't come right in to a Radical Challenge or Peak Rut Calling, you now have his attention and you can throw up a decoy, or try rattling, or hot cow calls, or maybe some soft mews, or a couple of glunks – anything to bring that bull the rest of the way in.

The following chapters deal with those imperfect situations that defeat 90% of the bowhunters, such as hunting in the early season before the rut begins, solving the problem of a hung up bull, a retreating bull, a silent bull, and a herd bull. These chapters will help you solve these problems and catapult you to the exalted level of advanced elk hunting. For it is the experienced archer, with his advanced knowledge and expertise, who relishes the challenge of the next encounter, even when a successful hunt is counted as coup, rather than a dead bull. And that's why we call it hunting.

As various hunting fraternities, such a rifle and muzzleloader hunters, vie for adequate hunting time, archery seasons are being pushed back into late August when the bulls are not bugling consistently. In spite of this, many smart bowhunters have solved the early season bowhunting problem and are killing big bulls.

Chapter 7

SOLVING THE PROBLEM
OF EARLY-SEASON ELK HUNTING

The large five-point bull vigorously raked his mighty rack of antlers against the lodgepole sapling until it had been reduced to a skinned, limbless pulp. The bull paused to sniff the pungent aroma of oozing pitch as the first rays of late August sunlight filtered into the dense northern Idaho forest.

Only days before, this bull had gingerly rubbed the velvet from his antlers, but already he'd demolished several young trees, and the urge to demolish other things rose as he grew more and more testy. Strange yearnings and delicious urges momentarily scorched through his body, and he had begun sniffing after passing cows for some telltale sign of estrus.

Suddenly, a bugle sounded from an alder brush thicket 150 yards away. The bull wheeled around and listened intently. Another bugle sounded, then another. Several cows began to call from that area, followed by another bugle.

The bull extended his neck and emitted a low, hoarse squeal – his first weak attempt at bugling since he'd become hard-antlered. Immediately, an answering bugle erupted from the alder patch. Then another bugle sounded, then another. Cows cried out, followed by a cacophony of bugling. Driven by his erupting mating instinct, the bull stomped forward to investigate the commotion.

The bull picked up his pace as he approached the alders because the bulging and calling had risen to a feverish pitch. As he trotted into a small opening in the alders, a loud cow call sounded from below. The bull stopped and looked down at a strange form beside a bush fifteen yards away.

A moment later, an arrow struck the bull's chest, and the startled animal galloped into the forest for 100 yards before collapsing. Within minutes I stood admiring the magnificent animal at my feet. Not only was he a dandy trophy, he was also further proof that elk hunting can be very productive for the bowhunter who has mastered early season elk hunting techniques.

As various hunting fraternities, ranging from muzzleloaders to rifle hunters, vie for adequate hunting time, many archery seasons are being pushed back into late August. All too often, bowhunters are finding the hunting very difficult during this early part of the season because the elk rut has not yet begun in earnest and the bulls are not bugling consistently. And those few bulls who do begin bugling early, don't respond well to a bowhunter's calling.

In spite of these problems, there is a rapidly growing number of archers who have solved the problem of early season elk hunting. And they're not only taking elk, they're taking big bulls!

Like my hunting partner, Walt Morkert, who is one of the best archery elk hunters I know. Walt states, "I prefer to hunt when the rut is just getting started because the big bulls haven't rounded up their harems yet, but they're getting testy and combative. I've brought in and killed several big bulls early in the season that would have been herd bulls later on and tough to hunt after they'd rounded up their cows. But when I slipped into their stomping grounds early and challenged them, they came right in to look for the intruder. Later in the season, after everybody's been calling at them, you can't hardly get one of those big bulls in."

There are three ingredients to solving the problem of early season elk hunting: understanding the biology of the elk rut, effective early season calling, and locating bulls in the early season.

Elk Rut Biology

A bull elk begins to prepare for the rut as soon as his new antlers appear in spring. They serve no useful purpose other than to establish each bull's place in the upcoming rut, still months away. During this time, nourishing calcium fibers and phosphate are carried to the soft bony tissue by tiny blood vessels that corkscrew their way up through velvet-covered antlers.

Through the summer months the bulls live in large bachelor groups away from the cows. During this period, the pecking order becomes established, with the larger bulls, who will become the future herd bulls, showing dominance over the lesser bulls.

By late August, a bull's antler growth is complete, and his body emits a small amount of the male hormone, testosterone, from the bull's testicles. This hormone travels in the blood to the base of the elk's antlers and blocks the flow of blood to the antlers, effectively killing them. The dead bone quickly hardens, and the bull immediately rubs the velvet from his antlers.

From that moment on, a bull elk is biologically capable, and more than willing, to mate due to the rapidly increasing levels of testosterone flowing through his body. The problem at this time is the cows. Until a cow comes into estrus, successful mating is not possible. Normally, a cow elk comes into heat in mid-September. However, I've seen cows in heat as early as late August.

Early Calling

The bowhunter who can fool an early season bull into thinking that "something" may be happening nearby stands an excellent chance of getting that elk to investigate.

My Peak Rut Elk Calling technique, which is covered in Chapter

A bowhunter who can fool an early season bull into thinking that something exciting is happening nearby stands the best chance of getting that elk to investigate.

3, works very well on these early season bulls.

Here's the condensed theory behind peak rut calling. When the peak of the rut occurs, the action is frantic. Bulls everywhere are bugling and chasing cows, who are calling out to keep track of each other. That's exactly what I try to simulate with my calling. I'll emit a long bugle, followed by a short grunt. Then I'll turn the bugle away and bugle again, making it sound as if it came from a different position.

Next, I'll emit several loud cow calls, followed by another bugle. I normally keep up this feverish bugling for about five minutes. Then I stop and listen intently for a few minutes before repeating the process. Usually, any bull in the area cannot resist investigating this sudden commotion in his backyard.

I've seen guys try to juggle several different calls while performing this multiple calling procedure. They spend more time searching for the proper "spike bull" or "lead cow" mouth diaphragm than they do searching the forest for elk. I use only a mouth diaphragm and grunt tube, which I can easily tone down to sound like a young bull, then bellow out a mature bull's bugle, followed by several soft cow mews – all with the same diaphragm. I may throw a few hot cow calls in, followed by some seductive mews. Heck, I may even do some clacking with a rattling box to simulate two bulls engaging in a friendly pushing match.

Now a word of caution: If a bull doesn't answer your calling, don't get up and leave. Early season bulls are notorious for coming in silently. Always plan to sit tight for about fifteen minutes after your last call.

Locating Bulls

The big problem with early season elk hunting is locating the bulls. The animals are not yet very vocal, so it's often difficult to find those areas where the bulls are hanging out around the vast western forests. In addition, bulls who are in the early stages of the rut tend to stay put and usually won't travel a long distance to investigate a bowhunter's calling, no matter how enticing it may sound.

The best way to locate rutting bulls is to hike along a ridge line, glassing for elk in openings and bugling off both sides. You can cover a lot of country during a morning or evening hunt, and often times, you'll locate more than one bull.

However, the most response you may get from an early season bull on a ridge 400 yards away is a single grunt. But that's enough! You

In early season, don't expect elk to bugle back a furious reply to your calling. A bull may respond with a single grunt, but that's enough to pinpoint his location.

now have the bull's location pinpointed, and you just need to slip forward to the general area where the bull had called from and get into position.

I never begin calling without studying an area thoroughly and deciding from what direction and through which particular opening an incoming bull will appear. This is necessary because an early season bull may stomp forward without bugling.

I learned that lesson the hard way early in my elk hunting days. I'd been bugling at a bull who had answered me from a ridge 200 yards away. Finally, the bull quit bugling, even though I'd repeatedly challenged him. After 10 minutes of no response, I grew restless (and disgusted!). I stood up and was about to leave, when I heard a branch snap to my right. There stood the bull, eyeing me in alarm. The elk whirled and disappeared into the forest, leaving me sadder, but wiser, about the approach of a silent bull.

There will be times when you bugle into an area that should harbor several bulls, but no response is heard. It is not unusual for a bull to ignore a distant bugle in the early stages of the rut. If I get no response after bugling into a particularly promising area, I'll slip down the smaller finger ridges where the elk are most likely to live and I'll search for rubs.

Elk tend to roam much farther than deer, but usually if you find several rubs on a ridge, there is a good chance that a bull is living nearby. One rub doesn't mean much to me, but if I find three or more rubs strung out along a ridge, it's been my experience that it's an area favored by a bull elk, and I then formulate a hunting strategy for that bull.

When Calling Is Out: Non-Rut Strategies

Besides calling, there are three other productive early season elk hunting methods: stalking, wallow/water hole sitting and trail hunting. Any one of these alternative methods can be used when over-hunting has the elk spooked and tentative toward answering calls, or on a rainy day when you don't want to get soaked covering miles of rugged forest, or early in the season if you cannot coax the bulls to bugle. After a few days of hunting hard, or if your feet become sore or blistered, you might be wise to sit along a trail or over a water hole. It would be a productive way to spend an evening while your body heals.

Stalking

In areas where elk are bombarded by calls from hunters, the animals tend to become very call-shy. They'll squeal out an occasional response, but stay hidden in small pockets of cover until nightfall.

Unlike the furtive deer, elk are not overly cautious or suspicious when they are in their security cover. A bowhunter can often stalk undetected right into such cover and in the middle of a herd of elk. Any noise you make while moving forward will be dismissed, and sometimes even acts as an attractant if you emit an occasional cow call. The elk will think you're just another cow who has come over to join the herd.

In the very early stages of the elk rut, the bulls may be just in the process of turning hard-horned and rubbing the velvet off their antlers. During this period, a bull may be hesitant to call to a distant peak rut calling tactic. It's been my experience that you sometimes have to penetrate within a hundred yards before a bull will respond. If I'm relatively sure that elk are in a particular area, but they're not vocal, I'll still-hunt specific areas of prime elk habitat – such as a secluded meadow that shows recent signs of elk feeding, or a pocket of timber where I think elk may be bedding. I'll slip through these areas, occasionally cow calling softly.

A few years ago, I arrived in Colorado for the first day of elk hunting season, but my friends assured me that the elk were not vocal yet. I found this to be true after a half dozen calling setups from various

When the bulls aren't vocal, it's a good idea to still-hunt into those areas where you suspect they are hiding, then begin calling softly to get a response.

ridge tops. So I targeted a series of gently rolling ridges and draws at the head of a shallow basin. I began moving slowly from ridge to draw, softly cow calling while searching for fresh tracks and rubs.

I stopped on a small aspen covered ridge and cow called about a dozen times. I heard cows calling in the draw ahead. Then I heard what sounded like a muffled grunt. I hurried forward and kneeled behind a small aspen tree and emitted a very soft bugle. Nothing. I cow called a few more times, and the cows started answering me again. I bugled again, and a very soft, hoarse bugle floated out of the draw.

I scooted ahead to the brow of the ridge and bugled. The bull responded with a low bugle. We went back and forth a few times, and then I saw the bull, a decent five-point, emerge from the timber and cross the creek below. It was obvious from the way his head was up and swiveling back and forth, that he was looking for the other bull who had invaded his comfy domain. He passed below me, and I cringed because the wind was blowing right at him. At the last second, the breeze switched to a cross wind, and the bull stepped into the open at sixteen yards. I shot him low in the chest and he galloped away, but I heard him cough and fall below me about sixty yards. Back at camp that night, my friends were astounded when I brought back proof that at least one bull had been ready to start rutting.

That wasn't the first time I've used this stalking tactic successfully on an opening day bull. I remember one opening weekend in Montana when the western jet stream sent a blast of scorching desert heat north. Temperatures were in the mid-nineties. It's the first time I ever embarked on a wilderness elk hunt in the dark – in a camouflage t-shirt! Absolutely no one was bowhunting that first weekend, so at least I had the woods to myself.

As I hiked uphill in the dark that first morning through a grove of knee-high huckleberry bushes – in a t-shirt and still sweating profusely – I was astounded when a bull grunted about eighty yards to my right. Then I heard the snap and pop of huckleberry brush. The bull, having heard me crunching through the brush, must have figured I was another elk. He was coming to investigate. Before I could execute a proper retreat (remember, it was still dusk), I saw a huge set of elk antlers floating toward me. I hunkered down behind a two-foot bush and tried to hide, but the bull stopped twenty-five yards away, threw his nose into the air, and trotted off. Sometimes, that's all it takes in the early season to get a bull to come in. They're just beginning to feel those delicious, confusing rutting urges, and they're apt to respond to anything unusual in their domain.

Wallow and Water Hole Sitting

Early September in the West is usually hot and dry. The elk seek out springs, water holes and marshy areas so they can escape the heat and insects. They paw out shallow depressions, then wallow in the cool mud. Wallowing not only helps an elk escape the heat, but the mud pack on its body also protects it from the bites of blood-thirsty horseflies. Eventually, a wallow will reek with the musty odors of visiting elk, and it becomes a gathering place for the elk. Bulls in the early stages of the rut especially like to visit a wallow and sniff the tepid water for the delicious odors of cows.

In the more arid areas of the southern Rockies, water is a precious commodity, and an the elk herd's life is tied to water holes, which they visit daily. If you locate a water hole, hunt it. My friend and Bowhunter Magazine editor, Dwight Schuh, drew a coveted elk tag for Arizona, and he told me of his hunt, "If you found water in the area of Arizona I was hunting, you killed an elk the first evening. I stumbled upon a small wallow hidden in some junipers while scouting one afternoon, so I

Montana resident, Joe Egan, used a decoy at this marshy water hole to bring down this dandy bull.

returned that evening. I don't think I was there a half hour when I heard a bull bugling as he came toward me. That bull walked right up to the wallow, and I shot him at fifteen yards. He scored 330 points."

It's different in the northern Rocky Mountains, where numerous gushing streams are found in every drainage. The elk can cool off just about anywhere, so wallows are less important, and hunting one is chancy. In Montana, I once found a hot wallow along a boggy creek bottom with the water freshly churned up and fresh elk tracks everywhere. I fashioned a crude blind, and I sat there and sat there. After three evenings of seeing nothing I gave up, and as I was working my way downhill, I found another wallow, then another, and another. There was so much water on that hillside that the elk could create an instant wallow any time they felt like getting a cool mud pack, and they did not have to return to any specific location.

When you find a promising wallow, check the wind direction, then set up a brush blind on the downwind side of the main game trail leading into the wallow, and sit tight. Elk usually become nervous and edgy when approaching a water hole because they've learned that an occasional hunter or large predator may be lying in wait. They'll stop forty yards away in the open and mill around, until a single cow ventures forth. If that cow doesn't become alarmed, the entire herd will come forward in a frolicking, splashing mass, and that's when the bull will show himself.

My friend, Dan Evans, drew a permit for a coveted tag in one of New Mexico's trophy elk hunting areas. The state offered two seasons, early and late. Dan didn't like either date, but he chose the early hunt, which was the first week in September.

Dan's fears proved real when the weather continued hot and dry, and the bulls remained vocally nonexistent. Dan had heard about a water hole located about three miles to the north of his camp, so he set out early one afternoon to find it. The water hole was located at the mouth of a small draw at the base of a rugged, rocky mountain. Dan fashioned a crude blind and had just settled in when another bowhunter showed up. Dan offered to leave, but the guy good naturedly shook his head and said, "I've sat here the last two evenings and nothing came in. I think I'll go still-hunting this evening."

Dan settled back in, but didn't feel overly optimistic after listening to the other bowhunter's assessment of the water hole. The elk were probably wary and came in only at night.

About forty minutes later, Dan heard another bowhunter walking behind him. That's it, he thought, there's just too many hunters around here. Then he heard a branch snap. No bowhunter would make that much noise! He peeked around a tree and spotted a cow elk standing about fifty yards away, suspiciously eyeing the water hole.

Dan tunneled into the sparse brush and remained still. Other elk began milling around behind him, and finally one brave cow cautiously stepped into the water. A few seconds later, the entire herd thundered into the water hole. Dan enjoyed watching the cows splashing and calling, but he was a bit disappointed that there was no bull.

He heard a loud grunt to his right and spotted antlers moving through the pinon pine. A huge bull stepped to the edge of the water hole, studied the relaxed nature of the cows in the water, then stepped in and began guzzling water.

But Dan now had a serious problem. A cow had ambled over and spotted him in the brush. She was standing stiff-legged, body tense, head high and drawn back – a typical alert pose. The other elk noticed the edgy cow and they also began milling around nervously. The bull suddenly went stiff and warily eyed the cow.

Ever so slowly, Dan raised his bow, praying that his movement would not spook the cow. Amazingly, he was able to draw and place his 30 yards sight pin behind the bull's shoulder. The arrow hit perfectly, and the entire elk herd exploded in a huge splash of water. When the commotion finally settled down, Dan slipped over to the other side of the water hole and found a heavy trail of bright, frothy blood. He found the bull piled up seventy yards away.

The bull was a large six-point that later scored 335 points. Dan said, "There were only two other bulls taken in that unit that I know of. I like calling elk, but at that time of year and in that heat, calling wasn't working. I've never killed an elk at a water hole. Frankly, I kind of enjoyed it."

And here's an interesting fact that you don't want to overlook: elk seldom look up! This means it's a smart idea to bring along a tree stand on your hunt. If a tree is handy near the water hole or wallow, by all means hang your stand and hunt from it, if the wind direction is right. The tree-stand elk hunter has the advantage of keeping his scent above the elk while being able to see the surrounding terrain better, and he can get away with more movement above the sharp-eyed elk.

Anyone who hunts elk in an arid area where water hole or wallow hunting is a possibility, should bring along a decoy. When elk approach such a place, they become very cautious and wary that a hunter or large predator, such as a mountain lion, might be lurking nearby. As soon as the elk see another cow at ease, they lose their wariness and come forward. A cow elk decoy will accomplish this. (See Chapter 4 for more specifics about decoying.)

One of the nice things about using a cow elk decoy at a wallow or water hole is that you don't have to rush to get the decoy set up in a good spot, like you normally would when a bugling bull is approaching. By arriving early, you'll have plenty of time to study incoming game trails and wind direction before you quietly set up your decoy.

Trail Hunting

Much of elk country is rugged terrain, so the elk use a trail system to travel between feeding, bedding and watering areas. They often use these same trails every day, and the smart bowhunter will, too. There are two ways to hunt a trail in elk country. You can set up an ambush along a well-used game trail, or you can still-hunt along a game trail until you spot an elk, then either ambush or stalk it.

In dense cover, the elk tend to use the same trails every day, so you may want to set up a brush blind or tree stand downwind of a trail.

Much of elk country is in rugged terrain, so the elk use trails extensively to travel from feeding to bedding areas. Bulls can often be ambushed along these trails in the early season.

In more open terrain with multiple trails, still-hunting along a main game trail works very well. Slowly move along a well-used trail and glass the meadows and parks ahead for elk. If the animals are feeding in a meadow, you can then stalk forward for a shot, or you can hurry over to the trail where the elk are traveling and set up an ambush.

At times, the elk are vocal only in the morning during the early part of the season, probably because of the warm temperatures common during that first week or two. Bulls will bugle in the morning, providing passable rutting activity, but the afternoon bowhunter will find only silence in the elk woods. Consequently, some guys stay in camp in the evening, but I've found excellent trail hunting at this time. I've also benefitted by staying close to the elk, and when there's a sudden upsurge in rutting activity late in the day, I knew exactly where to be headed the next morning.

The early part of elk season is considered a waste of time by some bowhunters who complain about hot weather, lack of elk activity and an absence of bugling. But for the aggressive bowhunter, early season elk hunting is an excellent opportunity to engage those bulls before they become call-shy. Don't sit home that first week and miss out.

A bull often hangs up just out of range when he arrives at the area where the calling has been coming from, but sees no elk. An elk decoy will often solve this problem.

Chapter 8

SOLVING THE PROBLEM OF A HUNG-UP BULL

You've done everything right. You located a rutting bull and enticed him forward with a selection of calls. The wind is in your face. Your ambush site is set up so the bull will pass by at fifteen yards. Everything is perfect, except for one thing. The bull stops fifty yards away. You whine and wail and plead to him with a selection of seductive cow calls and bugles. As a last resort you pray. Nothing works. You have a hung up bull.

It's enough to drive you mad. In the midst of hundreds of square miles of wilderness, a coveted bull elk stands just fifty yards away, and he won't come any closer. It has, and undoubtedly will in the future, happened to me. And I hate it. It's enough to make you doubt your calling ability. It gives you an inferiority complex. It makes you want to jump up and run screaming at that *&%#@$ bull and show him who's boss!

I don't have all the answers to solve the problem of a hung up bull, but I do understand some of the reasons why a bull hangs up, and I've developed hunting techniques that will often lure a stubborn bull those extra few yards into bow range.

Why a Bull Hangs Up

A bull elk is prone to hang up for a variety of reasons – some apparent, others more subtle. One of the most apparent reasons why a bull hangs up is the absence of an elk in the area where he heard an elk calling from. This is a common mistake inexperienced elk hunters make. They locate an opening, hide behind a bush, and begin calling. The bull stomps forward and surveys the opening, but sees no elk, so he bugles and rakes his antlers and tears up the ground. Having spent his frustrations, he feels justified and stalks off, leaving the bewildered bowhunter to wonder what he did wrong.

The cow elk decoy was invented for exactly this type of situation. When that bull spots the elk decoy, his suspicion and fear dissipates, and he usually continues forward. Chapter 4 covers decoying in detail.

But if you don't want to pack around a decoy, and you enjoy the one-on-one challenge of an elk encounter, like I do, you have a problem. You must be two places at the same time – out front to shoot the bull as he comes in, and back where the calling is coming from. You can solve this problem by "throwing" your calls, and seeking denser cover for your ambush site. To throw your call, you simply turn away from the incoming elk when you bugle or cow call. It will sound to the bull like your call is coming from the area behind you, and the bull will be less prone to hang up in front of you.

Of course, if you double team a bull, you'll solve all your problems, right? Well, not exactly. There are other, less apparent reasons why a bull hangs up. He might be at the fringe of his home territory and reluctant to leave it. A few years ago, I was bowhunting with Dennis Williams in Colorado. One evening we spotted a big herd bull and six

Bull elk tend to have a home territory where they feel safe, and they often won't leave it. That's why it's best to get as close to a bugling elk as possible before confronting him.

cows on an oak brush sidehill about 300 yards away. I hurried forward about fifty yards and hid where a well-used game trail crossed a small stream. Dennis began bugling, and the herd bull went berserk. He charged down that hillside, tore up trees, bugled up a storm, but no matter what Dennis threw at him (Dennis is a world champion elk caller), that bull refused to cross over to my side of the creek. I watched him for a half hour, strutting and bellowing sixty yards away, but he would not come closer. It was as if there was an invisible barrier on the other side of the stream. It became obvious to me that the bull had advanced to the edge of his territory, and was content to stand guard against the unseen intruder bugling at him. Finally, the bull stomped back to his cows.

I've seen bulls do this too many times to discount this territorial concept. They rush forward to confront an unseen challenger, advancing to some geographical point that may, or may not, be obvious, such as that stream. They tear up brush and scream a warning. Feeling justified, they stomp back to their thicket.

The obvious solution to successfully hunting this type of hung up bull is to present him with a radical challenge. At the time that Dennis and I encountered that big Colorado bull, we were working on an elk hunting video to show how far an elk could be brought in, and I knew we were passing up an excellent opportunity. If we had slipped forward about 200 yards and set up on the downwind side of that elk herd, then bugled, I believe the herd bull would have galloped forward a hundred yards to vanquish the trespassing bull, and I would have killed him.

I believe that the best way to avoid a hung up bull under any circumstances is to move in as close as possible and present him with a radical challenge. In doing so, you will have penetrated his territory and invaded his comfort zone. Herd bull or raghorn, he's prone to come looking for the unseen invader of his domain.

Occasionally, a bull will not come forward if he is an immature animal who has had a bad experience with another bull, or has been called to by other hunters. My son, Tony, and I encountered such a bull this past fall in western Montana. I'd already shot a bull, so I agreed to go out with Tony, who works two jobs and finds it difficult to take off the time needed for the back country treks his father enjoys.

We parked along a forest road near a side drainage just a mile from a busy Interstate. I'd heard a few bulls bugling in this small drainage the week before, but two bowhunters were hunting there at the time, and the area was too small for three hunters, so I left.

That morning, we hiked a half mile in the dark and arrived at the point of a high ridge above a series of small openings at the head of the basin. While we waited on a low ridge for dawn, a bull bugled near the farthest opening about 300 yards away and continued bugling every ten minutes. At first light, we advanced without calling because the bull's occasional bugling kept us on course. We halted about a hundred yards from the opening. We were in open lodgepole forest, so I whispered to Tony that we should drop down to where some alder brush and small red fir trees furnished more cover.

We slipped downhill a short distance, and Tony eased forward about fifty yards and set up behind a fir tree. The bull bugled about a hundred yards away. I sucked in a deep breath and bugled. Nothing. I waited a minute and bugled again. This time the bull answered, but from the same place. We bugled back and forth two more times, and it became obvious that the bull was not coming in. I guessed that he'd been bugled at and chased around by those two bowhunters the previous week.

Tony glanced back at me and shrugged. I scooted forward to him and whispered that we should ease downhill a bit and forward, then set up again, with both of us softly cow calling.

With Tony about forty yards in front of me and hidden behind a screen of alder bushes, I began cow calling. Tony answered my cow calls with light mews, and I answered back. The bull bugled from about eighty yards in front and above Tony, but I couldn't see him. After we cow called some more, the bull bugled from a position somewhat farther away.

My hopes sank. I began calling louder, throwing more insistent mews at the bull, hoping to beckon him back. I noticed that Tony had stopped cow calling. I thought, Gee, he could make things sound more realistic if he'd throw in a few cow calls once in a while.

A sudden crashing erupted ahead, and I saw the bull charge downhill through the trees. When he gathered his feet to jump a small creek, I noticed that he stumbled before he leaped across it. Hmm, I thought, could something have happened between Tony and that bull? And was that the reason why Tony had quit bugling?

Tony shuffled back to me, and from the big grin on his face, I knew he had a story to tell. "Well, Dad," he began, "I quit bugling because I saw the bull out in front of me kinda circling below, and the trees are really thin out there. I was in plain view of him, so I decided to stop calling. He seemed so intent on your cow calls that I thought it would be best to keep his attention focused back in your direction.

"Every time you'd call, the bull would huff, as if he wanted to

Mike and Tony Lapinski with the fruit of their joint effort.

bugle, then he'd trot forward a couple steps and listen, but he seemed a little spooked, too. For a while it looked like he'd walk away at about fifty yards, then you started wailing away and he turned back and stood about twenty-five yards away, but quartering toward me. He finally turned broadside and I shot. The hit looked pretty good. I'm surprised he made it across the creek."

We walked down to the creek and found bright red blood with tiny air bubbles, signifying a lung hit. A short distance up the other side of the draw we found Tony's bull. He was a far cry from record book size, but Tony was very pleased with his bull. And it was truly a trophy experience for this father.

My take on this entire hunt is that we encountered one of those call-shy, furtive young bulls that are most prone to hang up after having been exposed to other hunters and maybe a few bigger bulls by the middle of the rut. A radical challenge did nothing to bring this bull forward. Fortunately, I had a hunch that this was a young bull who might not want to take any chances, so I took the precaution beforehand to set up where cover would allow us to set up in another place if we had to – away from the bugling – and re-engage the bull with soft cow calls, maybe make him think a few cows have slipped away from the bull who was calling to them. My plan worked perfectly, and it might have worked even if Tony had been hunting alone, though he would have had to throw his cow calls back to entice the bull to move past him.

When you encounter one of those hung up bulls, and there's enough cover between you and the bull, try moving in a circle route downwind and try a completely different type of calling. I've even had success just raking a tree with my Rake & Brake call. It's a different sound that is not loud or threatening, and a few hesitant bulls have responded.

Things change dramatically when a bull hangs up within sight of your ambush. You lose the luxury of being able to circle to the side and set up in a different place, like Tony and I did with that young bull. The good news is that there are still a few tricks that will get a hung up bull in to bow range. I've brought two hung up bulls trotting forward when I quit bugling and cow calling and went strictly to a hot cow call. The sudden change in tone seemed to excite both bulls, and they came forward quickly. I must mention, though, that another bull trotted away when I began calling to him with a hot cow call. That bull was a smallish raghorn, and my guess is that no call was going to entice him to come forward.

I once even killed a hung up bull without calling. The bull stopped in a small red fir thicket about fifty yards away and began raking his antlers on a tall sapling. I started rubbing a tree to provoke and prompt him to stomp forward to rout his challenger. Instead, the bull rubbed and rubbed, and I watched in fascination, then frustration as the top of that bushy fir tree whipped back and forth. And then it hit me: That bull can't see anything with his snout stuck into that limby sapling.

Feeling totally exposed, I stood and took a few steps forward. The bull continued raking. Emboldened, I hurried to a stand of lodgepole pine trees fifteen yards away. The bull pulled his head back, turned away and bugled. I threw a short bugle back. The bull whipped around and began punishing the tree again. I eased forward, feeling strangely unsettled, and padded to a small opening, where I could clearly see the bull's chest heaving as he pushed against the small tree. I sent an arrow into his chest, and the bull jumped back and looked around. He started walking away, then his knees buckled and he went down.

Two years later I was an observer to an identical encounter, but with different results while I was the cameraman during an elk bowhunt in New Mexico's famous Valle Vidal trophy area. The bulls were big and boisterous, but we had a tough time following them through miles of rolling pine flats. One morning, the guide brought in a big bull that hung up about seventy yards away and began raking his antlers on a pine tree. The guide looked at me and shrugged. I motioned him to go forward and shoot the bull, who had his face stuck inside this branchy young pine tree and was whipping it back and forth.

Try to set up an ambush in cover so you can quickly readjust your position if the bull changes his approach.

But instead of moving forward quickly, the guide led the hunter on a painfully slow circuitous route. After ten minutes of tip-toeing, they had still not moved into bow range. Finally, the rising sun sent the wind swirling, and the bull jerked back, raised his nose into the air, and trotted away.

Back at camp, the guide breathlessly explained to the outfitter what had happened. The outfitter, an experienced elk hunter, gave the guide a ridiculous look and said, "Why didn't you just walk up and shoot him?"

Break Off and Try Again

Three different times, I've had bulls hung up for up to an hour, and I used those situations to see if an occasional bull would come in after such a long time. One time, I decided to break contact and try a second setup. I was hidden behind a tree on a narrow ridge, so I eased back out of sight, then trotted about 300 yards down the ridge.

I waited for about a half hour, then bugled. The bull bugled from across a small draw and halfway up the opposite sidehill. He'd traveled about 400 yards, and I guessed he was moving up to a dense stand of

If a bull hangs up, and it becomes apparent that something is bothering him, it may be wise to retreat and try to re-engage the bull in a different area.

stunted alpine fir trees on the ridge top to bed down.

I hurried across the draw about 200 yards downstream from where the bull had bugled and climbed as fast as I could to the top of the ridge, a distance of about 600 feet. I arrived at the ridge top soaked in sweat and gasping for breath. It was getting late, so I dared not take the time to cool off and rest. I turned away and bugled. I was startled to hear the bull bugle less than a hundred yards away. I hurried forward, the dense trees allowing me to move swiftly with little fear of being seen.

Ahead was a small opening in the tight-packed trees. I guessed that I was close, and was contemplating crossing the opening when I heard a branch snap. The bull was no more than thirty yards ahead. I hid behind a small hemlock tree and brought the bugle to my mouth, but I was in a quandary. Should I bugle or cow call? The bull had come in to my bugling during the last setup, but he'd also hung up, and all my cow calling had not brought him forward. And considering the fact that he was preparing to bed down, I decided to cow call.

I turned away and emitted a single soft cow call, waited about ten seconds, then called twice more. The bull didn't respond, but a jolt of adrenalin shot through me as branches snapped and hooves thumped on the forest floor. The noise was coming from right in front of me, but I still couldn't see the bull. I squinted into the brush, then looked above a small tree and spotted the tips of an antler not more than ten yards away. I dared not call again. It was a tense standoff, with the bull standing motionless and me sweating profusely as the sun-warmed wind began to swirl.

With sinking heart, I watched the antler tips turn away, but then they turned back and the bull stepped into the opening. Our eyes met for only an instant before I released. My arrow zipped right through the bull's chest, and he bolted into the brush, sounding more like an elephant as he crashed through the dense cover. Then I heard a cough, and I knew it was over.

I've broken contact with two other hung up bulls and was able to re-engage and bring them in later in a different area. One was a five-point bull that I brought back in and killed by using another radical challenge, and I used a mew cow call to bring in another five-point bull that winded me and fled. There have been a few instances, though, when I couldn't entice a bull back in after breaking contact with him.

I wish I had a surefire hunting technique, or some magical call or potion that I could pass on to you to solve your hung up bull problems, but I don't. However, I can state that my experience has shown me that a bull hangs up for a variety of reasons. Whether your setup or calling is what makes the bull hang up, or it's simply an unknown quirk of elk behavior, I feel strongly that a time clock is ticking, and you've got only so much time to change that bull's mind before he moves off.

You might try a change of calls, or a short dash to re-set up, or you might want to break off contact and try another setup. But I firmly believe that you've got to do something quickly because, with a hung up bull, he who hesitates is lost.

Chapter 9

SOLVING THE PROBLEM OF A RETREATING BULL

There is a BIG difference between a hung-up bull and a retreating bull. A hung-up bull has halted his advance, maybe just long enough to rake his antlers on a tree or do some dominance posturing and bugling before he continues forward. He's certainly still interested; that's why he's there.

A retreating bull, on the other hand, has sized up the situation and not liked what he saw, heard or smelled, and he's leaving. He's made the decision to break off contact for any of the above reasons, or for reasons known only to a bull elk.

But that doesn't mean a bull who breaks contact and retreats is unhuntable. On the contrary, I've killed more than a dozen retreating bull elk – some advanced almost to bow range before retreating, while others began moving away immediately after I called to them.. Both of these types of situations seemed hopeless at first, but by persevering and trying new hunting tactics, I've been able to take my share of these retreating bulls.

Why a Bull Comes Forward, Then Retreats

Some reasons why a bull might come forward, then retreat are obvious. Probably the number one reason a bull retreats from a bowhunter is that he becomes suspicious when he arrives at the area where the calling has been coming from, but sees no elk. As I mentioned in Chapter 8, a cow elk decoy will solve the problem of a suspicious bull.

But sometimes, a bull retreats for reasons that are purely human error. Several years ago, we were working on an elk hunting video in western Montana. The cameraman and I hiked into a back country area of the Anaconda Pintlar Wilderness area in southwestern Montana on September 14th. The rut had just begun in earnest, and we were greatly encouraged to hear three bulls bugling up ahead as we hiked along an open ridge as the first rays of sun splashed the mountains with a golden amber hue.

I decided to try for the bull nearest us, who was bugling from a dense stand of young fir trees across a small creek. The cameraman and I slipped across the creek (Note my comments in Chapter 8 about elk not liking to cross boundaries.) and onto a small ridge. The cameraman hid behind an overturned tree, where he was able to conceal his entire body. Only the camera lens would be visible between the V created by two roots. I hurried forward and hid behind a screen of snow brush.

I bugled and the bull immediately responded. Within seconds I heard hooves pounding and saw the flash of antlers coming through the trees. I remember that the gloating thought flashed through my mind: "This is going to be an easy kill."

I raised my bow when the elk was thirty yards away and began pulling back the string. The bull stopped. He looked past me for about ten seconds, then slowly turned and walked away.

I was dumbfounded! We were both well hidden, the wind was in our favor. What could have gone wrong? When I stood and turned back to the cameraman, the answer was obvious. The sun was glinting off the four-inch camera lens, resulting in a blinding mirror flash that had halted the bull and sent him in nervous retreat.

Gold-rimmed eyeglasses, metallic noise, or any other unnatural sound such as the swish of nylon can make a bull swap ends and ruin a promising hunt. Of course, there are even more obvious things that send a bull packing. A missed shot usually sends a bull back the way he came, but there are exceptions. I know of three instances when an arrow clattering in the trees from a missed shot spooked an incoming bull and he ran off, but when the hunter called, the bull responded and eventually came back and was shot. In these situations, the bull was hot and hadn't seen or smelled the hunter, and eventually ignored its instinctive urge to flee.

I had the same thing happen to me in Idaho several years ago. I'd called in a small six-point bull, but the top limb of my bow hit a branch when I released, and the arrow darted off to the right. The bull bolted, but ran just ten yards and stopped. When he turned broadside at twenty-five yards, I shot him, and he ran only forty yards before going down with a tremendous crash.

A retreating bull is a big problem because he has sized up the situation and not liked what he saw, heard or smelled – and he's leaving!

A bull that retreats after hearing, seeing, or smelling a bowhunter can be a very difficult animal to bring back in, and some experienced bowhunters opt to move on to another bull. However, I've had some success with spooked bulls who retreated at first. My rule of thumb is to wait about ten minutes, then call at the retreating elk again from another position. Most of the time, a badly spooked bull will move off and not respond to a call. If he responds and a heated discourse results, it's still possible to re-engage that elk.

Gold-rimmed eyeglasses, a metallic noise, or any other unnatural sound can make a bull swap ends and ruin a promising hunt. So will the clang of an arrow clattering through the trees from a missed shot.

Early in my elk hunting career, I had a disastrous initial encounter with an Idaho bull that taught me the value of persistence with a retreating bull. I was still-hunting up an overgrown logging road in the early morning, when a bull bugled about a 150 yards to my left and across a shallow draw. I set up behind an alder bush on the old road and bugled. The bull bugled back and I saw him coming through the trees. It was then that I noticed the wind at the back of my neck. I decided to move down the road to a bush thirty yards away, which would put me on the downwind side when the bull came in.

I was halfway there when I heard the pounding of hooves and looked up. The bull was standing twenty-five yards away, head up and alert. Then his nose wrinkled, and he bolted. I was disgusted with my lack of forethought, and I'd started walking away, when the bull bugled from across the draw.

"No way," I thought. "That has to be another bull." I bugled, and the bull answered with the same musical tone. It was the same bull. I figured, What have I got to lose? I trotted across the shallow draw and into a dense thicket of young cedar trees, advancing slowly until I guessed the elk was nearby. I bugled, and the bull shot back a reply from about sixty yards away. Back and forth we bugled. A branch snapped; antlers swished against trees limbs. I saw a tan patch moving to my left in the thicket and heard the grate of antlers against a tree. The bull was punishing a tree just twenty yards away. I eased to my right and found a small window to shoot through. My arrow rammed into the bull's chest and he ran off, but I located him a half hour later. He was a big nontypical 5X6 and my first Pope & Young record book elk. I wouldn't have killed that bull if I'd given up after he'd seen and smelled me.

When a Bull Retreats for No Apparent Reason

At times, a bull will retreat as soon as he realizes you are moving toward him. I've even had bulls retreat immediately when I called to them from long distance. These are the animals that are hard to hunt because you have no idea why they are moving away. When that happens to me, my guess is that they've had a bad experience with a hunter and are call-shy, or they've just had a run-in with a bigger bull. These are the most likely scenarios that occurred beforehand to send a long distance bull moving away even before he is pressured.

Of course, a herd bull will almost always move off when he realizes that another bull is closing in on him. There are specific ways to successfully hunt a herd bull that will be covered in chapter 11. The retreating bulls we'll cover in this chapter are those lone bulls who don't have the added complication of a harem of cows to deal with.

How To Hunt a Retreating Bull

The two best ways to hunt a retreating bull are: re-engage, or pressure. Which of these methods you use depends largely upon the reaction of the bull when you first make your presence known. At times, I've used one or both of these hunting methods on the same bull, again depending mainly on the opportunity created by the elk's actions.

Re-Engaging a Bull

A bull that stands his ground before retreating, or a bull who initially comes in to your call before leaving, can often be re-engaged in another area and brought in to bow range. It is not unusual for a bull to behave this way, especially when bugled at from a distance. A bull may respond by bugling and tearing up brush and trees, essentially performing a rutting ritual. Feeling justified with his pugnacious performance, he'll move off, but when re-engaged at close range, he may react more aggressively and come looking for his challenger.

Early in the season, before a bull has had a bad experience with other hunters or elk, I'm prone to move in close to him and confront him again with a radical challenge. But as the season progresses, and a bull is exposed to unknown conditions and situations that make him tentative and prone to retreat, I try to re-engage that bull with a different situation than the one he'd just walked away from. If he walked away from my bugling, I'll try cow calling . And if that doesn't work, I may try raking or rattling.

The biggest challenge for the bowhunter is to somehow manage to make close contact with the bull again. Usually, a bull will occasionally bugle even after he has retreated. Using this bugling as a directional guide, you can then move toward him. Hopefully, the bull will bugle another time or two to keep you on course. But don't call while you're moving forward because that's what made the bull retreat to begin with.

The two best ways to hunt a retreating bull are: re-engage, or pressure. The bowhunter who follows closely behind a retreating bull may eventually pressure the bull into coming back to rout his tormentor.

Three years ago I encountered two bulls on a mountainside, one high and the other low. I decided to pursue the bull located lower on the mountain because he was closer. This bull was bugling from a dark stand of timber where the elk normally bed. I moved forward and bugled at him from about a hundred yards away, but after the bull bugled twice, he moved off, bugling as he went. I considered leaving this bull alone and going after the other bull, but I'd already dropped a long ways down the steep mountainside, so I thought I'd give the retreating bull another try, especially since he was still bugling regularly.

I hurried forward until I approached a small ridge from where the bull had last bugled. At this point, I committed an error in judgment. Even though the bull had just retreated from my bugling, I guessed from the way he was still aggressively bugling, that he might come in to a different bugling setup. For a few seconds, it appeared I was right. The bull bugled twice from a thicket across a swale eighty yards away. I heard a branch snap and dove behind a blown down tree. But when I bugled again, the bull answered from 200 yards away and farther up the mountain.

I cursed my stupidity and hurried after him. He bugled twice more, each time on the move. I arrived, sweating, on a small finger ridge, and the bull bugled from just out of sight off to my left. It was a perfect ambush site, but the wind was wrong so I dropped below the ridge and circled. When I finally arrived at the far end of the ridge, the wind was in my face, but the bull by now was bugling from farther up the mountain.

Again I climbed and waited impatiently for the bull to sound off. When he bugled from the other side of a ridge about a hundred yards away, I dropped down to a marshy bottom and set up behind another blowdown. I began softly cow calling, then added more insistent cow calls. The bull came on the run, with his nose close to the ground in a prominent rutting gesture.

I barely got my bow up before he was in front of me, and I stopped him with a loud cow call. My arrow hit him low behind the shoulder and he let out a loud grunt before running off. I found him wedged between two trees, and it took me the better part of an hour to free the carcass, but I was very pleased that I was able to bring in this retreating bull. In retrospect, I believe that I could have saved myself a lot of time and energy if I hadn't bugled at him after re-setting up the first time.

As you can see from the above hunt, it's often a simple matter of using a different call or technique when re-engaging a bull, but sometimes just switching from a bugle to a cow call won't solve the problem of a retreating bull. One time, I followed after a bull, trying bugles, then cow calls, but he continued moving away. Finally, I climbed onto a ridge two hundred yards away from the bull and started wailing away on a hot cow call, throwing loud, insistent calls at him.

As I've mentioned, it's normally not a good idea to start right in with hot cow calls because you may send the wrong message – that a frightened cow is sounding off – but I was desperate to try something different. The bull responded with more aggressive bugles as I increased the pitch of the hot cow calls. Finally, he came forward at a fast walk, but caught my scent before I could get a shot and crashed off into the forest.

One more method that I've used successfully on a retreating bull is circling. After a while, it may become obvious that the bull knows you're back there, and as long as you stay on that direct line of pursuit, any call or hunting method you use will be ignored or viewed with suspicion by the bull. But in the meantime, there are other elk calling – a bull bugling on a far ridge, or cows across a draw.

You can fool a retreating bull into forgetting that you're behind him and make him think that he's happened upon something new if you quit your straight-line pursuit and circle on the downwind side. I'm not talking about getting in front of the bull and ambushing him. That's just about impossible with a swift-moving bull. With the circling tactic, you just want to present your hunting technique off to the side and away from that direct line you've been following. The circling tactic may sound easy, but it's not because you must hustle in a large circle and get set up before the bull is beyond close calling range.

I've successfully accomplished the circling maneuver several times, and it especially works well if you know the country and are reasonably sure where the bull is headed. One time I was following a bugling bull up a long ridge that led up to a saddle. I guessed the bull would eventually cross into the neighboring drainage through that saddle, so I dropped off the ridge, crossed a small creek below, and trotted ahead. I was about 150 yards from the saddle when the bull bugled about even with me. I felt I was off to the side enough to try a new set-up. I ran forward about sixty yards and hunkered down behind a bushy sapling. I cow called, and the bull bugled and started my way. He was a huge bull, one the biggest I've ever seen in the elk woods, and my hands trembled when I raised my bow.

Then a branch snapped behind me, and I turned around. An alert

The author re-engaged this five-point Colorado bull three times before finally drawing him in to 15 yards.

spike bull stood thirty yards away watching me. The spike's stiff posture stopped the big bull's advance, and a few seconds later the spike winded me and both bulls ran off. My plan had worked perfectly, and only the inopportune arrival of the spike saved that big bull.

Pressuring a Retreating Bull

At times, a bull will continue retreating no matter what new call or setup you try. And it's maddening. The bull remains interested, as evidenced by his bugling, but stays coyly out of range. With this kind of bull, I'll sometimes pressure him by moving forward quickly to surprise and confront him at close range. Sometimes this tactic works; sometimes it doesn't. And yet, I've been surprised how often this last-ditch tactic has worked on a bull that I had just about given up on.

One time in southwest Montana, I was following a retreating bull into the heart of a large back country basin. The bull was bugling up a storm, but continued moving away steadily. I tried a few setups with cow calls, but the bull didn't turn back, so I began moving in on him, peppering him with squeaky bugles. My intent was to make him believe that he was being confronted and offended by a smallish bull, and my hope was that he'd grow tired of retreating from the younger bull and turn back to confront him.

But nothing I tried worked. The bull stayed well ahead of me. At one point, I contemplated giving up on this bull because he was wearing me out as he headed farther up the basin, but I guessed that if he entered a brushy sidehill up ahead, he might slow down and look for a place to bed.

The bull entered the dense tangle of mountain ash, alder and vine maple. Up to that point, the bull had been retreating through open forest, making it impossible for me to get closer than about eighty yards without being seen. Now, I tunneled through the brush, heard the bull bugle about sixty yards ahead, and pushed forward even closer. I heard brush snapping just ahead, so I turned away and emitted a squeaky bugle. The bull's response was to begin raking his antlers on a tree.

I decided to match his challenge in kind. I put my bugle away and began rubbing a small tree with a large branch. A muffled growl floated back to me, followed by the crunch of hooves in the brush. For a few frantic seconds, I wasn't sure if he was moving toward me or away. Then a big mountain ash bush twenty feet in front of me parted as a large four-point bull shouldered into a narrow opening. He was just four yards away when I shot him.

It's not a bad idea to hold back if you are pursuing a retreating bull through open country because you run the risk of being seen if you move in too close. Wait until the bull enters an area where brush or trees obscure his rear view, and then move forward quickly. Your chances of turning that bull back increase greatly the closer you get before you re-engage him.

When to Give Up on a Retreating Bull

Taking up the challenge of a retreating bull is one of the most rewarding and exciting methods of hunting elk. There's a lot of satisfaction when you finally fool one of those fast moving bulls into swapping ends and coming back, but it's also an endeavor that's fraught with frustration, and sore feet and tired muscles. And a hunt for a retreating bull is never a sure thing. I've hunted many bulls who kept on going, and at some point I had to confess that the particular bull I was following simply was not going to turn back.

One reason why I have given up pursuit of a retreating bull is purely physical – when I couldn't keep up with that long-legged elk I'd been following. Another reason I've quit following a bull had to do with the hour of the day. If it's an evening hunt, and sundown is fast

Taking up the challenge of a retreating bull is one of the most rewarding and exciting methods of hunting elk. One of the keys is knowing when to pursue a retreating bull, and when to give up.

approaching, it may be best to break off the hunt, rather than run the risk of finally getting the bull to turn back, only to run out of shooting light. You also don't want to get caught away from your camp without adequate provisions.

Another problem occurs in the morning when thermal air currents, heated by the mid-morning sun, cause the air to swirl and virtually insure that the bull will catch your scent even if he turns back. One more problem that any bowhunter faces when pursuing a retreating bull is the possibility of ruining the next day's hunt. If you push that bull too much, he's liable to leave the country, but maybe if you leave him alone, he'll be more receptive to your hunting methods after a day of cow-less groanings. And while you're fruitlessly chasing after that bull, you may be alerting and educating other elk in the area. This is a difficult call to make at times, while impending darkness or a swirling wind make the decision easier.

When to Pursue a Retreating Bull

If a bull is bugling constantly while retreating, or acting agitated in other ways, such as growling and grinding his teeth, he's angry and may instinctively turn back to confront his tormentor. More than once I've pushed such a bull until I had just about convinced myself that it was a lost cause, only to have the bull swap ends and came looking for me. When this happens, a simple squeaky "teen-age" bugle thrown back behind you will do the trick.

Another reason I'll continue in pursuit of a retreating bull is if there is some geographical obstacle that will either slow down or halt a bull's retreat. A rock bluff ahead that halts a bull's movement will cause him to stop, which allows you to move in close and confront him. At that point, he may turn back to settle the problem behind him. Even a dense thicket will usually slow down a retreating bull, especially if it's late in the morning and he's tired and ready to bed down. That's when he's most likely to make a stand.

The retreating bull is one of my favorite elk to hunt. It is a bit exasperating at times, but it's always a pure adrenalin rush because you're constantly on the move, trying new calls, new gimmicks, anything to turn that bull back. It doesn't always happen. You'll lose your fair share of these intense battles, which makes you savor those occasional victories as very special moments in the elk woods when that big bull is lying at your feet. Because you harvested an animal that most hunters say is unhuntable. But not for you. In your mind, no bull is unhuntable.

Chapter 10

SOLVING THE PROBLEM OF A SILENT BULL

The 2001 elk archery season in Montana was excellent, with the bulls bugling on opening day September first. I almost killed a 300 class herd bull on the very first morning. I had the big six-point less than fifteen yards away, but he caught my scent just one step before he entered a small opening. It went like that just about every time I took to the woods – bulls screaming in my face.

But in spite of all this bugling, the five-point herd bull that I killed during the peak of the rut never made a sound. This bull provides a good example of what many archers are not aware of concerning silent bulls and opportunities lost.

On September 16th, I hiked through the early morning darkness into an area where a side drainage met two other draws to create a wide, secluded basin. Lots of feed and water meant prime elk habitat. Two large herd bulls had rounded up most of the cows. I hunted these herd bulls on successive hunts and came close to killing both, but the cows interfered with my plans.

That morning, I stopped to await the dawn about a hundred yards from an avalanche chute where I'd located the elk the last time I hunted the place. A bull bugled from farther up the basin, and another bull answered from across the basin. I recognized both calls as coming from the herd bulls. I waited until good shooting light, then hustled toward the bull on my side of the drainage.

But as I hiked, I wondered about something that had been bothering me since I'd begun hunting these elk. There were lots of cows, plus those two herd bulls, but where were all the satellite bulls? Were those two herd bulls the only ones in this drainage? I operate on the law

A silent bull is the bane of a bowhunter. You can do everything right and draw that elk right in, but if you're not aware that the bull is in the area, you're prone to give up the hunt too soon, step into the open, and come face-to-face with him. Curses!

of averages in elk country, and it just didn't add up. But I shrugged it off. I had too much to think about as I closed in on the herd bull.

As I approached another avalanche chute, I slowed down and studied the area ahead to avoid spooking any elk feeding in the opening. Nothing. I stepped into the opening and glanced down and across the creek. About two hundred yards away were three cows feeding in a small opening. Which I thought was strange. Normally, stray cows are quickly rounded up by the herd bulls.

Then I saw the body of a larger elk in the trees beside the small opening. I couldn't see the head, but the body was much paler than the rust colored fall coats of the cows. Only a bull would have a pale coat like that. But if it was a bull, why hadn't he bugled? Herd bulls bugle all the time, don't they? Then I reminded myself that I'd killed a big 5X6 herd bull several years before, and that bull hadn't made a sound until I'd stumbled into his cows.

The herd bull at the head of the basin bugled again about 200 yards away, and I hustled forward, but soon encountered cows. Before I could engage the herd bull, the milling cows had me surrounded, and one finally caught my scent and barked, which ended that hunt.

Which was fine with me because I was intrigued by the situation back in that small opening across the creek. I backtracked down the basin until I got the wind in my favor, then crossed the creek and eased forward. I heard the cows mewing, heard elk walking and stomping, but I never heard a bugle. I was still not sure that a bull was present. The only evidence I had was the pale body I'd seen through the trees. But I had a hunch there was a bull somewhere close by.

As I neared the opening, I saw a big cow with a body pale enough to be the animal that I'd seen earlier. I saw another cow above me, and a cow stepped into the opening below me. Then I heard an elk walking beyond a small screen of brush behind me. I was surrounded, with the possibility of my scent finding an elk at any moment. I knew this hunt would end very soon, and I feverishly pondered my next move. Should I bugle? I quickly vetoed that idea. If a bull was in the area, he wasn't interested in bugling, and I feared he'd retreat. Cow calls wouldn't work. The cows were already chirping constantly. And a sudden hot cow call might send the wrong message to the elk herd.

If a bull was nearby, it would have to be the animal I heard walking behind me, so I slipped forward and set up behind a small red fir sapling, then turned to face the direction that I thought/hoped the bull would come from. If, indeed, there was a bull. I pressed the Rake &

Brake grunt tube against the bark of a lodgepole pine tree and began turning it. A brisk grating sound filled the woods. Nothing. I'd hoped my simulation of a bull raking his antlers would prompt the bull to bugle, but the woods remained quiet, and I began to doubt that a bull was with these cows.

I glanced back and shuddered when I noticed that one of the cows had come forward to investigate the sound and was eyeing the red fir I was hiding behind. Then I heard hoof beats coming from the direction I'd hoped the bull was at, but I noted with dismay that the hoof beats had a casual beat, unlike the purposeful sound usually made by an incoming bull.

And then I saw the tan body, and a moment later the flash of an antler. A smallish five-point bull slowly walked through the open forest, head up, searching. He looked both angry and wary as he stepped forward and surveyed the area ahead. Meanwhile, the cow behind me had come closer, and I was feeling her eyes boring into my back. The bull began a painfully slow advance in a line that would bring him right by my ambush site.

I slowly raised my bow in anticipation of taking a shot, but I was also resigned to the fact that a kill was far from assured because the wind was blowing toward the bull, plus the cow behind me was beginning to act nervous. The bull stopped at thirty yards, quartering toward me, and looked directly at me. I didn't move and closed my eyes to avoid eye-to-eye contact.

To my amazement, the bull continued walking, but was acting more cautious. He'd seen something he didn't like, but he wasn't about to give up those cows just yet. When his head passed behind a small bush, I drew back. He stepped into the open and stopped about fifteen yards away. He turned his head toward me, and at that instant my arrow buried deep into his chest. He almost fell, regained his feet and charged off in a spray of dirt and twigs. Through the open forest, I could see him stop about seventy yards away, take a few steps and falter, then he dropped.

While I boned out the bull, I had plenty of time to think things through. My bull was not the biggest bull in that drainage, and my guess was that one or both of those bigger herd bulls had put the run on him, but with so many cows milling around, he'd been able to round up his own small harem. Content with things as they were, this bull turned mute to avoid catching the attention of one of the other herd bulls, or a bigger satellite bull. And as I was packing out the first load of meat, I bumped out two cows from a bedding area, and a small four-point trotted after them. I'd encountered two silent herd bulls in the same drainage.

A silent bull is the bane of a bowhunter. You can do everything right, and even draw a bull in, but if you aren't aware that a bull is in the area, you're prone to give up the hunt too quickly, and the result is usually an embarrassing, maddening encounter with an incoming bull the moment you step into the open because you hadn't heard anything. It's happened to me many times, and I hate to admit it, but it probably will happen again.

How often do bulls come in silently? I estimate that over the years about a hundred bulls have come in to my calling without uttering a sound.

How often does a bull come in silently? After rummaging through the cobwebs of my mind, I figure that about a hundred bulls have come in silently to my calling over the years. And those were only the one I knew about. What about all those unseen animals that had crashed off?

One time we were videoing a bowhunt in Oregon about hunting herd bulls. As we followed a retreating herd bull up a forested ridge, no less than three other satellite bulls shadowed us, with all of them coming forward silently to check out my calling. In two days of hunting that herd bull, only once did one of those satellite bulls make a sound, and that was just a soft grunt.

What I am saying is that there are a lot more bulls that respond to a bowhunter's calling than most guys realize. And it's not just those early season bulls, whom we expect to be quiet because of the early stages of the rut. As with my bull, it might be the peak of the rut when you encounter that silent bull. For that reason, a bowhunter should be aware of the hazard of bringing in a silent bull any time he puts a call to his mouth in the elk woods, and he should understand why a bull might choose to remain silent.

Why a Bull is Silent Early

Silence among the elk herd is common early in the season, especially if the rut has not begun yet, or is in the early stages. A bull responds vocally more and more as the testosterone increases in his system. Some bulls are reluctant to begin bugling, for whatever reason, even when they begin showing other rutting tendencies, such as raking their antlers, wallowing, or sniffing after cows.

But remember, just because an early season bull doesn't bugle, that doesn't mean he can't be called in and killed. I've already related several instances when I brought in bulls as early as the last week in

Master elk vocalist and guide, Paul Brown, told me, "Early in the season, and I'm talking the first of September, a silent bull is the rule, rather than the exception, and a bowhunter should approach every setup that way. In fact, I expect an elk to slip in silently whenever I start calling."

August. The bull elk hunting gospel according to Mike Lapinski is that any hard-antlered elk can be called in.

My friend, Paul Brown, agrees and is one of the leading proponents of early season elk hunting. Paul told me, "Early in the season, and I'm talking the first of September, a silent bull is the rule, rather than the exception, and a bowhunter should approach the hunt that way. In my opinion, this is the chief reason why so many bowhunters don't kill bulls. They give up the hunt because they blow on a bugle or cow call and don't hear or see an elk. They translate that to mean that either they aren't calling correctly, or the elk aren't interested. So they give up in disgust and walk back to their vehicle while a silent bull is working his way forward to check out who called.

"It's happened to me so many times that I absolutely expect an elk to show up whenever I start calling. I've bowkilled lots of bulls and brought in many bulls for clients. And a lot of them came in silently. More than once, I've had a client start fidgeting after I'd called for fifteen minutes without any action. The guy'll place his arrow back in his quiver and start to rise, but I'll make him sit back down. And five minutes later here comes this bull quietly sneaking in."

How To Hunt a Silent Bull Early

To successfully hunt a silent bull early, I'll again quote master elk guide Paul Brown: "Ya just gotta believe!" Paul simply means that when you set up and call correctly, you have to believe that an elk will respond, even if it's early in the season and the elk are not vocal yet. No, Paul doesn't bring in a bull every time he sets up, and neither do I. But we've both brought in enough silent early season bulls to know that we should stick around long enough to make sure some bull isn't coming in silently. And that means taking about a half hour during each setup to allow a bull to come in because early season bulls are notoriously slow moving in. And after the calling is finished, wait about ten or fifteen minutes to see if a bull might be coming in. Hey, it's early in the season! What's the hurry? If the bull's aren't vocal enough to help you pinpoint one, where are you going to rush off to?

Personally, I find early season hunting to be very exciting. Let's face it, anyone who stumbles upon a rut crazed bull can bring it in. But when the elk are silent, and the weather is hot, and everybody has gone home in defeat – that's when I take up the challenge. And I've brought home many nice bulls, to the consternation of my bowhunting friends who'd given up the hunt.

Most of my early season success with silent bulls is attributable to the Peak Rut Elk Calling technique. Many times, I've entered a drainage where I knew there were elk, but none were vocal until I sent a barrage of bugles and cow calls echoing through the mountains.

Early Season Setups That Work

There are two calling setups that work well with shy early season bulls. My Peak Rut Elk Calling method works very well to convince a bull that a cow has come into heat and is available just ahead. Most of my early season success is attributable to Peak Rut elk Calling. After a half hour of bouncing bugles and cow calls off the mountains, it's time to move to another area, but don't get in a rush. Wait a while to see if a silent bull may be sneaking in because, strangely, it's often during the silence following a sudden outburst of calling when one of these bulls comes in. I can't explain why. They just do.

I've also fallen into the habit of still-hunting away from a call site. More than once I've encountered an incoming bull who was meandering in my direction.

Another calling setup that works well is strictly cow calling, which is one of Paul Brown's favorites. Paul uses soft cow calls and slowly increases the volume, and he may eventually throw in a few hot cow calls. After a half hour, he sits and waits. "You'd be surprised," he says with a laugh," what's come in after I was done calling and was just sitting there."

There are other early season hunting methods that will also bring a bull forward, but most of them require a bowhunter to penetrate the elk's stomping grounds and make his presence known. I do this a lot. I'll enter a suspected elk feeding or bedding area, and cow call softly while moving slowly and listening for hoof beats because the bulls are usually going to come in silently to find out who's there.

One time I almost killed a rutting opening day bull elk in Montana, and neither man nor animal emitted a sound. At first light I slipped into a secluded meadow where I'd seen elk feeding during a scouting trip two weeks before. The meadow rimmed a small alpine lake nestled against the base of a sheer rock cliff just below timberline. I began still-hunting a game trail along the edge of the meadow, occasionally cow calling and staying to the timber to avoid being seen.

Above the gurgle of a small nearby stream, I became aware of a strange sound. For a minute my ears strained to pick up the unusual sound. And then it hit me. It was the sound of antlers grating against wood.

A jolt of adrenalin shot through my body, and I eased forward to a small spruce tree and kneeled. I picked up a dead limb and began rubbing the tree. The bull didn't bugle, but I heard a loud sigh come from a dark pocket of spruce trees fifty yards ahead.

The unseen bull began raking his antlers again, and I took that opportunity to slip forward about ten yards to twin white fir saplings, putting me just forty yards from the bull.

I lightly rubbed a sapling with the branch. Ahead, limbs snapped and popped, and I spotted the bull pushing through a tightly packed stand of young spruce trees. I brought my bow up, fully expecting to kill this animal, but a cow barked behind me. The bull halted, offering a quartering frontal shot, which I would never (and neither should you) take. The cow barked again, and then the bull spotted me and bolted. Whereupon, I swore vengeance upon that 8%$#@ cow and spent the better part of the next hour trying mightily to kill her. Only an opportune (for her) swirl of the wind saved that cow's life.

As I mentioned in Chapter 7, you can also successfully hunt silent early season bulls by lying in wait and ambushing them along main game trails, or still-hunting and stalking them when the trails become numerous, or setting up on a wallow or water hole. Whatever you do, don't sit at home during this early season. But if you do, don't be surprised if I (or some other wise bowhunter) don't knock on your door to show you the bull I just killed while you were lying on the sofa watching a football game on TV.

Why a Bull Is Silent During the Rut

A bull elk will turn mute during the rut for three reasons. The first reason is fear. Any bull who has contact with a human and runs away is almost surely going to shut up. This is a bull who's seen or smelled a bowhunter, recognized the danger, and is headed for the next county. I've related a few instances when I was able to get a few such bulls bugling and even brought them back in and killed them. Anything is possible if you don't give up, but practically speaking, your hunt for that bull is finished when he runs away from you.

The second reason a bull will become silent is intimidation. A raghorn bull, after having been pummeled for getting too close to a herd bull's cows, or chased all over the woods by a berserk mature satellite bull, may decide that the best way to escape a set of antlers being rammed up his young butt is to keep quiet. The majority of silent bulls fall into this category. They roam the elk woods, listening to the ebb and flow of the calling around them, and they might even try to sneak in and grab a wayward cow that wanders away from the big herd bull, but they are not going to risk pain and injury by vocally making their presence known.

The third reason a bull may become silent is frustration. While most herd bulls and mature satellite bulls become more vocal as their rutting frustrations increase, some bulls clam up. I've bowkilled two herd bulls who were actively guarding their harems and running off other bulls, but they weren't bugling. It was the nearby satellite bulls who had drawn me forward, and only then did I become aware of the big herd bull. One of these bulls didn't bugle, but he growled and clicked his teeth in anger after I'd sneaked in close to his cows and bugled.

One time while I was photographing rutting elk in Canada's Banff National Park, I spotted a huge bachelor bull raking his antlers on an aspen tree beside a small meadow. I slipped forward and took pictures as he tore the sapling up by the roots, then demolished a lodgepole pine tree that was four inches in diameter. The bull went from tree to tree, reducing each to pulp while bulls bugled all around him, but he never made a sound.

And then he spotted me. His head jerked back. He studied me for a few seconds, and a low, guttural growl rumbled from deep within his chest. He dropped his head and stomped toward me. I hastily climbed a tree. The bull stood inches away from my five thousand dollar telephoto lens and tripod and shook his antlers at me. It wasn't the first time that one of these rangy Canadian bulls had put me up a tree, so I wasn't overly concerned.

I waited until the bull stomped off and climbed down. I was rounding up my camera equipment, when I looked up and saw the bull coming at me again, this time on the run. I barely made it up the tree ahead of the bull, and this time I waited until he was a hundred yards away before I climbed down. I quickly grabbed my gear and headed in the opposite direction, but when I looked back, I was shocked to see the bull hurrying after me again. I shimmied up another lodgepole pine tree and sat there – tired, my arms scratched – and waited this time until the bull stomped out of sight over a ridge before I came down.

The above animal is a good example of a rut crazed bull who is so frustrated by the unrequited fire of lust in his loins, that he is beyond bugling. Such a bull is easy to call in and kill, but only if you are aware that he's out there. All it takes to kill such a bull is to make your presence known with a bugle or cow call.

One time I took a video cameraman along with me on a bowhunt into western Montana's Anaconda Pintlar Wilderness area. We parked at the end of the road at noon and took our time wandering about two miles up a trail along a knife ridge. We finally sat on a log and rested, soaking up the sun of a beautiful Indian Summer day, and we even discussed maybe taking a nap. And why not? It would be several hours before the elk were up and moving, and besides, we'd heard nothing on the way in.

The cameraman stretched out on a bed of bear grass and used his pack as a pillow. I pulled off my boots and sat back, soaking in the sun. I was content just to be in God's great creation. I picked up my bugle and brought it to my lips. At mid-day on a warm early afternoon, my sole purpose for bugling was to harass my cameraman. I blew a loud bugle, ending it with a series of grunts.

The cameraman chuckled and started to say something when a ferocious bugle ripped through the air from up the ridge about a hundred yards. The cameraman bolted upright, scrambling for his gear while I threw on my boots and nocked an arrow before jumping off to the side of the trail and kneeling down. The cameraman had no sooner positioned himself behind me then the bull came stomping down the trail. I raised my bow and cow called. The bull halted and looked at me an instant before I sent an arrow through his chest. The bull galloped off the ridge, but piled up about a hundred yards below in a jumble of blowdown.

We were stunned. We hadn't even begun hunting yet, and we already had a video bow kill. I jokingly called our good fortune divine intervention. The cameraman laughed and replied, "Whatever it is, Lapinski, you must be living right."

That's how easy it is to bring in one of these frustrated silent bulls during the peak of the rut. I've had several similar incidents occur through the years, when a bow kill amounted to me calling once, then hastily raising my bow and shooting a rut-maddened bull elk as it stood at point-blank range. But you have to be willing to get out there, even when no elk are bugling, and move through elk habitat while calling. You never know when a bull like the above animal will come charging forward.

How to Hunt a Silent Peak Rut Bull

The best way to provoke a silent bull during the peak of the rut is with Peak Rut Elk Calling. Many times, I've entered a drainage where the elk were not bugling in mid-September, but after fifteen minutes of peak rut elk calling, the hills were ringing with the squeals of bull elk. I believe the fevered pitch of numerous calls bombarding a silent, brooding bull in rut has the effect of tripping his emotional trigger.

A bull may respond with intense bugling and come in that way, or he may bugle just once and come in like the midday bull I mentioned above. Or he may come stomping forward, full of fight, but remaining silent. An immature bull, on the other had, often remains quiet, while timidly coming forward.

The key to bowkilling a silent bull is to "always" be ready, whether it's the first day of the season, or the peak of the rut. You don't know what state of mind an elk just out of sight is in, and you have no idea what effect your calling will have on him.

Here's a question to ponder. What about the elk that crashed off after you gave up the hunt last time you went afield? Just think, he might have been the trophy bull of a lifetime that would have been yours if you'd just waited a few more minutes. That's how easy it is to make or break your season – just a few minutes of patience.

Chapter 11

SOLVING THE PROBLEM OF THE HERD BULL

The huge herd bull raked his antlers on a spruce tree as a warning to the other bull who had moved toward his harem of six cows thirty yards away. Suddenly, the cows crashed off through the Colorado oak brush, leaving the big bull alert, but seething at their loss. Then a young bull bugled from the area vacated by the cows.

The enraged herd bull screamed a challenge and stomped forward to pummel the satellite bull who had just stolen his cows. As the herd bull stepped into a small clearing, a cow called to his right. The bull stopped and stared at the strange apparition kneeling behind a bush twenty yards away. A moment later, my arrow zipped forward and rammed into the monster's chest.

The startled elk galloped down the mountainside, but I heard him pile up about sixty yards away. I was there in a minute to survey my trophy. His long, chocolate brown antlers has six symmetrical points on either side, and I guessed they would make the record book. But much more than that, I had the satisfaction of knowing I'd successfully bowhunted an animal that most elk archery hunters consider unhuntable.

No doubt about it, the herd bull is the most difficult elk to hunt, but he's also worth the effort. He is the most coveted of trophy animals because it's usually a bigger, older bull who commands a harem of cows. And it is these older bulls who sport the massive racks that are the desire and object of every bowhunter who takes to the elk woods.

But to merely mention that the herd bull is difficult to hunt does not do justice to the enormous task any bowhunter undertakes when he takes up the challenge. Unlike lesser bulls, who come blissfully forward to a bowhunter's calls, a mature herd bull quickly leads his harem in the

The herd bull is the most difficult type of bull to hunt because he quickly leads his harem of cows away when a bowhunter moves in.

opposite direction and keeps on going. And why not? He already has what he wants!

If all that wasn't bad enough, numerous cows milling around the herd bull can provide a score or more of extra eyes, ears and noses. The cows may not consciously act as the bull's lookouts, but the effect is the same. It's often impossible to penetrate the outer defense of those sharp-eyed cows without alerting one of them. And then the hunt is over.

So, is the herd bull unhuntable? No way! Experienced elk bowhunters have discovered that even a wily herd bull has weaknesses, and by adapting your hunting tactics to take advantage of these weaknesses, you'll discover that the herd bull can be successfully hunted. And the more intimately you know your quarry, the more you can exploit his weaknesses. In my opinion, the key to harvesting a trophy-sized bull is understanding the role the herd bull plays during the rut.

The Dynamics of the Elk Rut

You don't have to read a three-inch thick biology book about the elk rut; you just need to know how the rut affects a herd bull. Depending upon the region, a cow elk comes into estrus for about forty-eight hours in mid September. Generally, the peak of the rut lasts about ten days, during which time all the cows will be bred. Though the bulls may be bugling before and after this peak-rut period, mating is impossible until a cow enters into her estrus cycle.

For about two days before a cow comes into heat, she exudes a pheromone that triggers the mating lust in a bull. The nearby bulls are all attracted to this cow, but it is the biggest bull, relying on either bluff or actual combat, who claims the right to mate the cow.

During this peak-rut period, the most dominant bull in the area will round up as many cows as he can control and chase away lesser bulls who try to sneak in and grab a cow. However, mature bulls from other areas who can't defeat the local herd bull begin to roam through the forest seeking cows. If the herd bull in the next drainage is smaller, the traveling bull will either bluff or fight the herd bull until one of them is vanquished.

For that reason, a herd bull has no interest in taking on every bull that bugles out a challenge. Instead, he'll quickly push his harem of cows away from a challenging bull who begins to move toward him. This is the scenario that causes so much frustration among bowhunters. A herd bull will answer their bugles all day at long distance, but when they move in, the herd bull moves away, and there are few bowhunters who can keep

If a herd bull thinks his challenger is getting too close and is about to slip away with his cows, he may swap ends and make a furious rush to rout the bull.

up with a long-legged elk.

A Herd Bull's Weakness

There are two conditions, call them weaknesses, that will make a herd bull turn back. If the herd bull thinks his challenger is getting too close and is about to slip away with his cows, he'll swap ends and make a furious rush to rout the bull. In addition, a rut-crazed herd bull whose cows are not in estrus, and therefore can't be mated, will leave his harem momentarily if he thinks there is a cow in heat nearby, his plan being to herd her back to the harem and mate her.

All a bowhunter has to do to make a retreating herd bull turn back is adapt his hunting techniques to create these conditions. And while nothing is foolproof when it comes to the herd bull, I've used three hunting techniques to harvest eight herd bulls. These techniques are: splitting the herd, pressure calling and Peak Rut Calling.

Splitting the Herd

A herd bull cannot keep track of every cow as he pushes the herd through dense, rugged terrain. It's not unusual for a cow to wander off or even turn to join another bull. Though it drives the bull crazy to lose a cow, he has no choice but to continue moving the main herd.

As the herd straggles along, there is a real danger that another bull could slip in and run off with the cows. When this happens the herd bull usually turns back to engage the offending bull.

Actually, it's quite simple for a bowhunter to sneak in and split the herd. I usually stop bugling at the retreating herd bull, but continue following close behind. The herd bull will eventually slow down or stop if he's not pressed, and the cows are soon back to feeding.

I'll pinpoint the herd bull's location to make sure he can't see me, then charge into the middle of the cows and scatter them. The chaos of pounding hooves and elk crashing away through the brush sends the herd bull into a frenzy, but at the same time, he is unsure what has happened.

I conceal myself between the herd bull and the direction his cows ran. I then send a squeaky bugle and a few "glunk" calls toward the fleeing cows to simulate a young bull going after and tending the harem. (Chapter 4 covers glunking in detail.) The squeaky bugle and "glunks" drive the herd bull berserk, and he'll usually charge forward to rout the bull who has taken his cows. It's then just a matter of drawing back, emitting a loud cow call to stop the fast moving bull as he passes by, and making a killing shot.

I've killed several herd bulls this way. The key is to split the cows without being seen by the herd bull. If you can do that, you're almost assured of a shot at the herd bull. But be ready! I've had herd bulls about run me over just seconds after the cows crashed off.

Pressure Calling

At times, it is impossible to get close to the cows without being seen by the herd bull. When this happens, I resort to pressure calling. Essentially, pressure calling is vocal harassment of the bull until he can't stand the insults any longer and comes back to defeat his tormentor.

Of course, pressure calling doesn't work as long as the herd bull is moving his harem away at a swift pace. But the herd will eventually tire of being pushed, and if the cows happen upon a prime feeding area, they'll simply refuse to go any farther.

That's exactly what happened to me a few years ago on a video bowhunt in Colorado. I'd followed a five-by-six herd bull for about a mile through dense oak brush, but when the herd emerged into a lush

At times, it's possible to get close to a herd bull's cows without being seen, then pressure the bull into coming forward to confront the unseen bull threatening to take his cows.

meadow at the head of a basin, the cows began gorging on the rich grass, leaving the herd bull to angrily prowl back and forth like a warden. I couldn't get closer than about 150 yards without being seen, so I picked a good ambush spot and began pressure calling.

I threw bellowing bugles at the herd bull nonstop. After about a dozen bugles in just a few minutes, I noticed that the herd bull began glancing in my direction, pacing back and forth and matching me bugle for bugle.

I increased my bugling until I was calling about every ten seconds or so. The bull would bugle, rake a tree with his antlers, and then glance back in my direction with fire in his eyes. I began cutting off his calls with my own bugles, and this further incensed him.

Finally, he could stand the insults no longer. He left his cows and stomped toward my ambush spot. A few seconds later, I heard brush breaking and his large antlers swishing through the trees. When the bull stepped into an opening below me, I cow called and he stopped at about eighteen yards. I made a perfect shot, and the bull barely made it back to his cows before he dropped.

Fortunately, the Stoneywolf Video cameraman caught the entire drama on film, and you can see for yourself how effective pressure calling can be in the video, *"Archery Elk–The Dream Hunt."*

Pressure Calling with Cow Calls

An interesting variation of my pressure calling technique was passed on to me by my good friend and Martin Archery Pro Staffer, Dan Evans, who's taken several huge herd bulls. Dan hunts solely for trophy-sized bulls, which means he's usually matching wits with a rangy herd bull.

Dan told me that he chased one particular herd bull for two hours before it became obvious that his bugling would not turn back the fast moving bull. Then he got an idea. Maybe, he reasoned, if the herd bull thought that a hot cow was chasing after him, the bull might turn back.

He continued following close behind the bull, but switched to loud, wailing cow calls. The bull moved away for a while, but then turned back, intrigued by the mysterious cow who was dying to meet him. That huge six-point bull is now on the wall of Dan's trophy room.

A few other sounds you can make when pressure calling to a nearby herd bull is brush raking and "glunking". I especially like the Rake & Brake elk call to simulate a bull raking a tree because you can accomplish it with a minimum of movement, and anyone who's hunted a herd bull knows the hazards of too much movement around those sharp-eyed cows. One warning bark will quickly end the most promising hunt.

Bedded Herd Pressure Calling

If the herd bull does not respond to pressure calling, there is still hope. You can try a variation of pressure calling: Bedded Herd Pressure Calling. Here's the theory behind it. If the herd bull won't come forward, wait until the herd beds down, which it usually does in cover. That allows you to slip forward and get close to the bedded elk. This is a normally placid time for the elk herd, when cuds are chewed and the herd bull, exhausted from hours of rutting, wants nothing but to snooze. He certainly doesn't want to be harassed at this time of day, but that's exactly what you want to do.

Get as close to the elk herd as possible; start calling and don't stop. It's usually better if two guys are calling at each other from about fifty yards apart, which simulates two satellite bulls who have moved in close and are challenging the herd bull. Something about two callers seems to get the herd bull upset, and he's apt to get out of his bed long

After the cows have bedded down, they are very reluctant to get up and move. At times, a bowhunter can move in close to the herd and pressure the bedded bull into coming forward.

enough to chase his two noisy competitors away.

And don't forget to try some rattling. I mentioned in Chapter 4 that I once watched a herd bull leave his cows and tromp a hundred yards to vanquish two young satellite bulls who were engaged in a friendly pushing match. A combination of madcap calling and intense rattling, in my opinion, would be hard for a bedded herd bull to stomach very long without reacting.

Peak Rut Calling

There may be periods of time during the rut when none of the cows in a herd bull's harem are in estrus. Sexually excited to the point of near madness, the herd bull roams among his cows, constantly sniffing them for the first signs of estrus. In this situation, the herd bull will leave his harem temporarily if he thinks a nearby cow is in heat.

When a cow is in estrus, nearby bulls begin bugling incessantly and call back and forth in their excitement. It's not unusual for a bull tending a hot cow to bugle a half dozen times in a minute. Added to all this is the loud crashing noises as these huge animals chase each other, and it becomes a wild, noisy time in the elk woods.

And that's where Peak Rut Elk Calling comes in. By simulating a peak rut situation nearby, a herd bull who has no cows in heat can sometimes be lured away from his harem while he tromps over to steal that hot cow for himself.

But remember, Peak Rut Calling also attracts other bulls. One time in north Idaho, I'd chased a herd bull through the dense brush for more than an hour until he took his herd into the middle of an alpine basin near the head of a draw. I could get no closer than 200 yards without being seen, so I began Peak Rut Calling. I bugled about twenty times in ten minutes, mixing in soft cow mews with loud, excited cow calls. Then I made antler raking sounds and even threw several large rocks through the brush to simulate elk crashing around.

The herd bull had begun matching my bugling and eventually moved toward me a hundred yards, but was still reluctant to leave his harem. Then a large five-point satellite bull came over a low ridge about 200 yards away. He ignored the herd in the meadow and hurried toward my position.

That spurred on the herd bull, and both elk broke into a trot as they rapidly closed in on me. I scooted to my right to set up an ambush – and ran right into another bull that had come up behind me through the brush. That bull ran off, and I barely made it behind a bush before the large satellite bull stomped into the far end of the opening about twenty-five yards away.

The elk halted and looked to his left at the oncoming herd bull, offering me a perfect broadside shot. The thermal air currents had begun to shift the wind direction toward the bulls, so I decided to take the shot. I sent an arrow zipping through the satellite bull, and he galloped off, but I heard him go down in a thicket behind me.

All the racket seemed to spur on the herd bull even more, but my decision proved wise when the elk suddenly halted about fifty yards away, sniffed the air for a few seconds, then bolted.

Silent Approach

Sometimes nothing works with a herd bull. They just keep moving away from everything you throw at them. When that happens you have two choices: give up or try the silent approach. I once killed a herd bull by keeping quiet because nothing I tried worked. I followed the herd to the head of a basin, where the cows began feeding, and I was able to slip in unnoticed, and I got a good shot at the five-point herd bull.

There may be periods of time during the peak of the rut when a herd bull's cows are not in estrus. At this time, a bowhunter using Peak Rut Calling may entice a herd bull to leave his cows long enough to snatch away the hot cow that is causing the commotion nearby.

There is no set hunting method when it comes to attacking a herd bull with silence. My friend, Wisconsin resident Bob Mussey, had an encounter with a big herd bull one morning in north Idaho that is worth mentioning. Bob had called and followed the herd bull until it holed up in the bottom of a brushy draw above the North Fork Clearwater River. Bob tried to provoke the bull with pressure calling, first using bugles, then switching to cow calls. The bull refused to budge, so Bob started easing downhill, hoping to split the herd, but a smallish raghorn bull started up to him. Bob feared that the bull would catch his scent and spook the other elk, so he hurried away.

Bob settled under a tree on the other side of the ridge because it was too late in the day to try another approach. He awoke at about 5:00 p.m. and studied the area where the bull had holed up. He was certain the elk herd was bedded in that bottom, but he was just as certain that the bull would move his harem away if Bob confronted him with more calling.

Bob decided to try to penetrate the elk's bedding area silently. The terrain was brushy enough that he figured he might be able to slip in unnoticed by the cows and get a shot at the bull. Bob worked his way down until he was about 200 feet from the bottom and entered a series of

Expert Wisconsin elk hunter, Bob Mussey, killed this big Idaho herd bull by using the silent approach.

brush thickets. The brush was perfect cover for hiding from the cows, but he was concerned about the noise he was making when he moved through it.

He heard a branch snap below him and to the right. Then he saw the large set of antlers. The herd bull was up and slowly moving toward him. Bob stepped back to a narrow shooting lane and waited. The bull's head entered the opening at about fifteen yards, and then his chest came into view. Bob's arrow smacked home, and after a short search, he found the big bull lying in a small fern glade.

Bob said of his hunt, "I don't know what made the bull come up to me. Maybe he'd just got out of his bed and decided to look for all those cows he'd heard in the morning, or maybe he heard me moving through the brush and came up to investigate. All I know is the silent approached worked."

If I had to choose one hunting technique that it is my favorite, I think I would choose Peak Rut Elk Calling because it signals to every elk within hearing range that "something exciting" is happening nearby and they'd better get over there in a hurry. It trips the emotional trigger, not only of a surly herd bull, but also any trailing satellite bulls. But there is also a rush of excitement when I split the herd, when I gather my feet and tense for the dash into the middle of the cows, splitting them away from the herd bull and most assuredly bringing a quick, angry reaction. And of course, it's just plain outrageous, obnoxious fun to bellow nonstop at an increasingly enraged herd bull with a barrage of pressure bugles. And as Bob Mussey just related, there are times when silence is golden.

Alas, not every hunt for the herd bull bears fruit, for to aspire to such lofty heights puts us in harms way and is fraught with hazards. A sharp-eyed cow, a fickle swirl of the wind – such simple things as these can foil our best laid plans. But if you are up to the ultimate challenge of elk hunting, and you are willing to adapt your hunting techniques to exploit a herd bull's weaknesses, that precious moment will surely arrive when the trophy of a lifetime is standing broadside in front of you.

Chapter 12

SOLVING THE AMBUSH SET-UP PROBLEM

I was at a large sporting show last winter when a young man from Oregon walked up to me, introduced himself as Jeff, and shook my hand. "Uh, Mister Lapinski," he said as a frown creased his brow, "I called in four different bulls using an Abe & Sons Estrus call, but I couldn't get them to come all the way in."

From that brief statement, I knew what the young man's problem was, but out of courtesy, I asked him to go on.

"Well," he continued, "the bulls came right in to the estrus call, but they all stopped about forty yards away and just looked at me. Then they walked off. I called and called. Nothing worked. I wish I'd brought my call along with me today. Maybe I'm not putting the right tone in it to bring a bull all the way in."

And the more that Jeff talked, the more apparent his problem became to me: His ambush set-ups were wrong.

Jeff told me that he was in his second year bowhunting. His first year had been a total bust while he wrestled with all the intricacies of elk archery hunting, but his second season was a breakthrough. He located a herd of rutting elk, and had been wise enough to purchase some good elk calls. He was absolutely astounded that he could actually bring in a bull elk all by himself.

"That first bull," he gushed, "was such an awesome experience, seeing that huge set of antlers weaving through the trees, and the big bull bellowing as he came in." Jeff's look turned sheepish when he added, "I was so shook up, I never even thought about shooting it."

Jeff's problem was obvious. He enjoyed watching the elk come in so much, that he set up his ambushes to have a ringside seat, choosing

A poor ambush setup that alerts an incoming bull is the number one reason for botched hunts by bowhunters.

his set-ups in an open area where he had a good view of the incoming elk. That single act, more than anything else, had doomed his hunts.

I hear this same lament at least a hundred times a year, with slight variations, and I quickly identify the problem – not with the calling, but with the set-up. And it doesn't take an Einstein to figure it out, either. For instance, Jeff's call's had worked well enough to bring the bull virtually into bow range, so it must have been something else that stopped those bulls.

I have this simple equation to deal with the process of bowkilling a rutting bull elk. The farther away the bull is, the more you can get away with. Conversely, the closer the bull gets, the less you can get away with. Think about it, you can call to a bull elk on a distant ridge in your underwear while dancing a jig and waving your arms. The closer that bull comes, the less you can jump around and wave your arms. And at some point, you're going to have to camouflage yourself and nock an arrow, and you're going to have to hide if you expect that bull to keep coming.

I realize the above analogy is kind of silly, but it holds an irrevocable truth: The closer that bull gets to bow range, the more critical every move becomes. We can look at this issue from the end and work backwards to prove it. The absolutely most important chore for a bowhunter to do is find his bow-killed elk, which is the culmination of having done everything correctly.

The next most important thing to do is to make a good shot, so the bull will die quickly, so the bowhunter will be able to find it. And the next most important thing a bowhunter must do is to get that bull into sure killing range by NOT doing anything to halt that incoming elk's advance.

You can take this line of reasoning all the way back to purchasing the correct equipment, but the irrevocable truth remains that the proper ambush set-up is the most important thing you'll do before you shoot your trophy bull. But in spite of its importance, many bowhunters don't give enough thought and consideration to this issue.

On the other hand, my first thought when a bull first answers my call is, "Where is my ambush set-up going to be if he comes in right now?" And if I move forward, immediately after I stop I'll survey the area for the best ambush site. In my opinion, there is a direct correlation between this train of thought and the forty elk I've killed over the years.

The importance of the ambush became apparent to me from the very start of my elk hunting career. Those first few bulls that I brought in from a long distance often came in on the downwind side, or beyond range and obscured by brush. It was very frustrating, at the time, to finally bring in a bull from 400 yards away, only to lose any chance of killing that elk because I wasn't set up where he came in.

The development of my Radical Elk Hunting Strategy changed all that. True, this new hunting method was very successful in aggressively confronting a bull at close range, but I also identified another benefit: By cutting down the distance between hunter and elk, the avenues that an incoming elk could take was lowered – often to a single trail or lane.

And THAT'S when I really began killing bulls – when the short distance traveled by the elk after a Radical Challenge eliminated the possibility that the incoming animal would come in on the downwind side, or beyond range, or in cover. As a result of my own experiences, plus those of hundreds of other archers I've interviewed over the years, I've determined that the key to setting up a killer ambush is to make it easy for the bull to come forward.

How to Make it Easy For the Bull to Come Forward

Besides being hesitant to travel a long distance to a bowhunter's call, a bull elk may not want to cross obstacles, such as a deep draw, rock slide or jumble of logs. I once made the mistake, while working on an elk hunting video, of setting up with my cameraman on the far side of a large blown down red fir tree. I liked the cover afforded by the small trees where I was at, and even though that big blowdown between the elk and I bothered me, I chose to stay put, rather than uproot the cameraman and risk being seen if we moved forward.

I bugled, and the smallish herd bull came looking for me. He came at a fast walk, bugling and searching for the other bull. He stopped about sixty yards away and began pacing back and forth. Each time I called, he'd swap ends. Back and forth he paced. It made great video, but after fifteen minutes, my heart began to sink. The bull was staying on the other side of that big blowdown. All he had to do was hop over it, and he'd be within bow range, but he was content to posture and bugle and keep the challenger at bay.

He finally retreated, leaving the cameraman happy with all the elk footage he'd shot, but leaving me frustrated by my mistake, which had cost me a video kill of a bull elk.

When you have a bull interested, test the wind, then survey the area for anything that might keep a bull from coming in. It may be something that's obvious, such as a rock bluff, or an item that's easily overlooked, like that downed tree with the Oregon bull.

The closer you can get to a bull before setting up your ambush, the less avenues the incoming bull has to stray from a course that will bring him into sure killing range.

At this point, you have a lot of latitude, even if the bull is coming forward. More than once, I've identified an obstacle for an incoming bull and hurtled a log or hopped across a small creek moments before the bull appeared. This simple chore leads to conditions that make an elk's approach easier to get into my bow range, which is the object of all the calling leading up to that moment.

Set up your ambush in an area where natural obstacles will not stop the bull from walking by you at close range.

Don't Back Up!

Don't back into an ambush. My son, Tony, learned this lesson the hard way a few years back. Tony had engaged a bull on a distant mountainside, so he moved down to the creek bottom, with the plan of crossing the creek and challenging the bull. After crossing the creek, he hurried across a small meadow, not much wider than thirty yards. But as he started up a game trail at the edge of the meadow, he heard branches snapping above.

"The bull was coming down looking for me," Tony recalls. "The edge of the meadow was a perfect spot to shoot the bull when he broke into the open, so I ran back to a spruce tree on the other side of the meadow. I'd have a twenty-five yard shot when the bull entered the meadow.

"Pretty soon I heard the bull coming. I saw antler tips first, then his head. He was a really big six-point. The biggest I've seen in the wilds. The bull came into the meadow on the trail I'd been standing on. I was just starting to pull back the string when the bull jerked his head back, snorted and charged back up the hill."

Later, I explained to Tony what he'd done wrong. He'd left his scent at the edge of the meadow, then backed up, allowing the incoming bull to catch a whiff of his scent on that trail. If Tony had moved forward to an ambush site, he probably would have killed that bull.

If you become aware that a bull is coming in, don't back up. You'll leave your scent exactly where you want the bull to be standing when you shoot him. If at all possible, move forward about twenty yards so the ambush site will be free of your odor.

Get On The Same Level With The Elk

In mountainous country, where most elk hunting takes place, I strongly suggest that you set up your ambush on the same elevation as the elk. Many times, incoming bulls have seen me when they came straight down a hillside, and the same thing happened when they came straight up. They just seem to have a height advantage that helps them to see up or down better, which allows them to pinpoint unnatural objects ahead.

A good example of this problem occurred during a thoroughly frustrating morning while I moved in on a herd bull in the Great Burn Wilderness in western Montana. When I got about 200 yards from the herd, a bull bugled above me. Before I could readjust my position, the bull was in view, stomping downhill at a fast clip. He stopped fifty yards away and eyed me hiding behind a skinny lodgepole pine tree. Not alarmed, but suddenly wary, he circled, caught my scent and bolted.

I shrugged off this botched encounter as an unexpected bonus. I hurried forward because the herd bull had moved off. When I bugled, another satellite bull called below me, and in a matter of seconds I could see him working his way up through a lodgepole pine thicket. Again, I had no time to set up a proper ambush, and the bull spotted me hiding behind two small pine trees. He turned and trotted off.

Now, I was a bit frustrated. Two bulls had come in within ten minutes, and I hadn't gotten a shot at either. The first bull that had come in from above, and winded me, never called again. But as I again moved toward the herd bull, the lower bull occasionally bugled.

The herd bull took his cows over a ridge and into a deep draw, probably to bed. I planned to dive off the ridge and go after the herd bull, but I hesitated on the ridge top. It was getting late in the morning, and the herd was a long ways down the other side and was maybe bedding down for the day. In the meantime I had a bull bugling below me that I could

It is important to get on the same level as the incoming bull in steep terrain to avoid being seen because an elk tends to pick out foreign objects better while looking uphill or downhill.

engage quickly. I pondered my options and decided that the bull below me, even though he'd trotted off after becoming suspicious, had continued bugling, and he was only a couple hundred yards away.

I swapped ends and trotted back about 300 yards, then dropped down to the same elevation as the bull. Instead of bugling, I decided to cow call because the bull might associate a bugle with the strange thing he'd seen hiding behind the small pines the first time he'd come in.

I eased forward to a short side ridge, and the bull bugled about 150 yards ahead. The forest was open in this area, with almost no cover to hide behind. I moved to an uprooted tree and kneeled behind the root wad. I tested the wind. It was still moving across the hillside and remained relatively steady, even though the sun was up and beginning to warm the thermal air currents.

Then I studied the area ahead. If that bull came in, he'd probably come on the ridge trail. And I was in a perfect position to kill him. I began cow calling, and the bull bugled, but didn't come in. I switched to hot cow calls and heard hoof beats coming from the mountainside above the ridge. The bull had moved up and was now coming straight to the cow calls, but not on the ridge trail. Then I saw him, weaving among blowdowns about seventy yards away.

I made a quick decision that I knew would make or break this hunt. I decided to move up the mountainside about twenty yards to another upturned tree root. But my problem was that the bull was in full view, and I had just a few seconds before he'd be in range. I watched the bull until he walked behind a large leaning fir tree, then I ran up to the tree roots and dropped down.

When I peeked out, the bull had halted. He stood with his head up, not appearing overly alarmed, but not at ease, either. He's seen or heard something. At that point, I figured my hunt was over, but then the bull snorted and dropped his head and started forward again. There was a narrow space between two large blowdowns, and the elk was headed for that opening, which would put him about fifteen yards away when he passed by.

Suddenly, the bull threw up his head and skidded to a halt about forty yards away. I checked the wind. It was still blowing away from the bull. But the bull's posture remained stiff and alert. He turned, and began walking away. Out of frustration, I bugled. Immediately, a bull bugled behind me. I slowly turned and spotted a large five-point bull walking up the mountainside right at me about seventy yards away.

At that point, I knew I was in trouble. The forest was very open, and I was in plain view of a bull above me and a bull below, and the sun was peeking through the forest. The bull below suddenly threw up his head and look at me, then at the retreating bull above, then back at me. Then he raised his nose into the air and sniffed several times before galloping back where he'd come from.

I slumped to the ground and surrendered. But as the sun's rays splashed over my face, I couldn't help but savor all the elk action from one morning's hunt. Four bulls within a hundred yards in the space of one hour! How could any bowhunter complain about that? However, as I headed back to camp, the thought occurred to me that my hunt was a good example of the hazards of calling a bull uphill or downhill, and I'd just run the gamut of them.

The above story also illustrates how much we are at the mercy of chance and circumstance during the course of a hunt, and how luck often plays a large part in our success, especially when unforseen elk encounters pop up. I could just as easily have killed an elk during any one of those four encounters, but only the last set-up gave me any real chance of killing a bull because I was finally able to control the set-up and create an ambush much more to my liking than the extreme downhill and uphill come-ins the first two times. True, that last set-up didn't result in a kill, but it was the surprise bull coming up from below that ruined that hunt, not the set-up.

Eliminate the Bull's Ability to Hear, See or Smell You

As you can see, these spur-of-the-moment set-ups are exciting, but often times serve only to raise your pulse rate and educate the elk. The most productive set-ups will occur when you eliminate the options of a bull to either see, hear or smell you, and that can best be done by getting as close in to the bull as possible, at the same elevation, and in a place where he'll pass by without being aware of your presence.

Because the Radical Elk Method is a close range challenge, it allows me to pick the place where I plan to encounter the bull. I often pick a spot that offers the bull just one travel route to get there, and I'm waiting off to the side for him.

In theory, every ambush set-up works perfectly, but we don't live in a perfect world, and we can't always have the cards in our favor. At times, you'll move in close to an unsuspecting bull who is rutting just out of sight, and the set-up site is perfect, but the wind may be dangerously close to blowing your scent to the elk. If you want to engage that elk and kill him, you're going to have to move to the side and catch a cross wind.

The bull halted, head up, not overly alarmed, but not at ease either.

Any set-up where the wind is "iffy" is destined to defeat you. Many times, I've moved over to the side to catch a more favorable wind and discovered that the new set-up site was just as good, and sometimes even better.

As I move in for a radical challenge, I constantly check the wind by sticking the tip of a finger into my mouth and raising that finger above my head. Even the slightest wind current will make that side of the finger feel cold. If the wind is adverse, I'll alter my normally straight-line advance so that when I get within 100 yards of the bull, the wind is in my favor, even though I may have been forced to make a big circle.

Plan your ambush in cover adequate enough to hide you, but sparse enough to allow you to monitor the bull's movement and give you clear shooting lanes.

Plan Your Ambush In Adequate Cover

Once I get about a hundred yards from a bull, and there's not enough cover to get closer, it's time to choose the place where I'm going to ambush the bull. If I have a choice, I'll move to an area that affords the most cover. Not a dense thicket, but with enough cover to hide in and allow for some unseen adjustment, if necessary. Remember the bowhunt with my son, Tony, in Chapter 6? We had that bull a hundred yards away in an open lodgepole forest, but I chose to move downhill about fifty yards to a place where some brush hid us better. Later, when that bull hung up, we were able to make a quick adjustment because the brush hid our movement. That decision to set up in cover, ultimately, is what allowed Tony to kill that bull. A less exposed ambush site also works to keep the bull from hanging up when he doesn't see an elk where all the calling had been coming from.

In very thick cover, such as the dense, brushy forests of north Idaho and western Montana, the problem is the opposite. The cover is so dense that you look for a small opening, instead of cover. Dwight Schuh told me that a few years back he was hunting northwest Montana, and several times he had big bulls within twenty yards, but couldn't get a shot. "One big bull came in to twelve yards," Dwight mentioned while shaking his head. "That bull stayed there and bugled for fifteen minutes, and I never got a shot at him."

Call me crazy, but I like to hunt the dense forests along the Idaho-Montana border because encounters are always close, and my shots average about ten yards. I've killed bulls as close as three yards in those jungles of brush. When I move in on a bull in dense cover, I will slip in a close as possible (I've moved to within thirty yards of a bull before challenging him). And I do it quietly. I want that bull to be surprised when he hears a call so close. After I move as close to a bull as I dare, I check the wind, then look for an opening, or a crease in the brush that I'm pretty sure the bull will move through to get to me. At such close range, the bull usually comes in exactly where I had planned. What a thrill it is when that bull comes by so close you can reach out and touch him!

Of course, if you are double teaming a bull using a decoy, you can afford the luxury of setting up in a more open site because the bull's attention will become riveted to that cow elk decoy, and even if the shooter doesn't have a great place to hide, he's less likely to be spotted because the bull's attention is on the decoy.

I believe that many bowhunters are good enough to bring a bull in to bow range, but they fail to kill the bull because they purposely put themselves in harm's way just so they can see that big bull coming in, as the young man did at the beginning of this chapter. Once I pick an ambush site, I'll also pick the spot where I'm going to shoot the oncoming bull, and I then stay out of sight off to the side. In fact, when that bull shows up, I stay hidden, rather than rise up and expose myself.

In the past, my impatience has led a bull, who may have been hunted and was suspicious as he came forward, to halt when he saw some part of me exposed. Now, I hunker down once I see the bull coming, and I just watch the tips of his antlers as he comes forward, safe in the knowledge that if I can't see his eyes, he can't see mine. When the bull gets within thirty yards and passes behind a screen of trees or brush, I'll rise up and draw my bow.

Often times, a bull passing by twenty yards away is moving too

Often times, some quick in-field adjustment is necessary if the bull does not advance through the shooting lanes you'd planned.

fast to shoot. I always cow call, which stops the bull and allows me to take a better shot. At this time, let me state that elk "usually" don't jump a string. If you are at full draw and ready to shoot before you cow call, rarely will a bull bolt. But if you cow call and then draw back while the bull is looking at you, or if you stand there at full draw for several seconds, that bull may very well bolt when you release.

A few years ago my son, Tony, called in a young bull, and as I videoed him, he drew back and cow called. The bull stopped at twenty yards, and Tony took his time shooting. In those three seconds, that bull spotted danger, recognized danger, and reacted to danger. Tony, normally an excellent shot, was astonished when his arrow zipped an inch over the bull's back. Later that evening, we ran the tape in slow motion and discovered why. The film showed the bull slowly begin to drop down and turn away as the arrow moved into view. By the time the arrow got there, the bull's chest was well below the arrow's flight.

In-Field Ambush Adjustments

Half the elk I've killed were the result of proper set-up, and they ended with a quick kill. When everything went right, the scenario went something like this: I heard the bull, moved forward to cut down his travel lanes, got the wind in my face, picked a good ambush site and hid off to the side. The bull came forward and I shot him. End of story.

But the other twenty elk I killed resulted in some sort of in-field adjustment. Sometimes, it's a simple thing, such as moving over to a better bush to hide behind, or moving forward to shoot the bull before he reaches a previously unseen obstruction. At other times, an in-field adjustment required extensive adjustments.

Here's a good example of how extreme an in-field adjustment can get before that bull is in the proper position. While working on an elk hunting video, I was peak rut elk calling one evening from a ridge into the head of a basin in Colorado's Wind River National Forest. I expected the elk to be in there somewhere, feeding on the lush grass of a small meadow which I knew was located about 300 yards ahead on my side of the draw.

A bull began bugling from directly across the draw. Soon, he was on my side of the draw and coming up to me. I whispered to the cameraman, "Our scent is blowing directly down to that bull. We're gonna have to get the wind in our favor." We ran down the ridge about 200 yards and dropped off the side. I called, and the bull bugled from the area I'd just vacated on the ridge top. As I mentioned, I don't like a bull to come straight up or straight down on me, so we huffed back onto the ridge. I called again, but in the meantime, the bull had stomped down to where I'd bugled the last time (bulls usually don't move so extensively when bugled at.).

I still didn't like the idea of that bull coming up to me, but after noticing the cameraman gasping for breath in the thin high country air, I decided to take another look around. I noticed a small level area below the ridge, and we moved down to it. I bugled, and then heard brush snapping. The bull stopped on the other side of a large mountain maple bush I was hiding behind and began raking his antlers less than five yards away. I turned away and bugled, and the bull stepped into the open to look up at the ridge top. I shot him and he ran into the basin. I heard him cough twice then fall. (You can see this bowkill in the video *Tips & Techniques of Elk Hunting.*)

I've related numerous encounters in this book when I've had to make in-field adjustments ranging from a move of only a few feet, to actually breaking contact with a bull so that I can circle around and re-engage him under more favorable conditions. And yes, some of my hunts have ended abruptly when an incoming bull spotted my movement. That's one of the hazards of aggressive elk hunting; it's also the reason we aggressive elk hunters kill so many elk while the more careful archer is still hiding behind some bush hoping that, by some miracle of nature, a distant bull will cross a mile of rough terrain and miraculously stand broadside at twenty yards.

The Don't's of Ambushing Elk
•Don't hide in an open area where a bull will center his attention on you.

•Don't expose yourself to get a better look at an incoming bull.

•Don't consider a set-up if the wind is swirling.

•Don't set up in open forest if a nearby site affords better cover.

•Don't call when the bull is near enough to pinpoint your location.

•Don't make an unnatural noise as the bull moves into bow range.

•Don't be afraid to move if it becomes obvious that the incoming bull's route will not afford a broadside killing shot.

•Don't move if the bull is looking directly at you. (He may decide that you are no danger and continue forward.)

•Don't set up an ambush above or below a bull, even if the wind is in your face. Move to the same elevation and settle for a cross wind.

The Do's of Ambushing an Elk

•Do seek an area where cover will allow some last second adjustments.

•Do seek an ambush site off to the side of the incoming bull's path.

•Do stay out of sight to avoid being seen when the bull is in plain view.

•Do adjust your ambush site if the bull's route does not afford a broadside shot.

•Do expect to circle if wind direction or terrain hamper an adequate ambush site.

•Do move to the same elevation of a bugling bull on a steep mountainside to avoid being seen when the elk comes straight down or straight up to you.

•Do use a decoy when hunting with a partner in open terrain.

•Do avoid noise when the bull is nearing bow range.

•Do quit calling when the bull appears, to avoid having your position pinpointed.

The shoulder blade of a bull elk is massive and extends beyond the back line of the foreleg. It is fully capable of stopping an arrow's penetration. For that reason, you should aim about a half foot behind the foreleg.

Chapter 13

SOLVING THE PROBLEM
OF PROPER SHOT SELECTION

Much of the information which I have imparted about the subject of elk hunting comes from my extensive experience and research, plus the information that I glean from other archery hunters. Men such as Larry D. Jones, Dwight Schuh and Paul Brown have shared a wealth of knowledge about elk hunting because of their extensive experience. But I've also been able to glean valuable information even from the novice elk bowhunter. Unfortunately, this info usually falls into the category of "How Not to Do It." So it is with a touch of sadness, and a twinge of frustration, that I will now pass on some sobering statistics concerning proper shot selection.

During a recent two year period, I studied the shooting habits of more than twenty elk archery hunters at various elk camps. These men ran the gamut from novice bowhunter to experienced, world-traveled sportsman.

First, the good news. Thirteen elk were shot while I was in these two camps. This was due to the large elk herds where these hunts took place, the increased elk activity during the rut, and the expertise of the guides.

Now, the bad news. Of those thirteen elk that were shot, only two were retrieved. And those two were my elk. I questioned each shooter in-depth, and I also queried the guide about the situations and conditions when the shot was taken. My findings could fill a book titled, "How Not to Shoot at a Bull Elk." And it didn't seem to matter whether the shooter was a beginner or an experienced bowhunter. Both made bonehead errors in judgment and took shots that shouldn't have been taken.

It's enough to drive me nuts. It keeps me awake at night. I've written a hundred articles in a score of magazines about how to hunt elk, and specifically, about how to kill one. Yet nobody listens – or it seems that way. At the large sportsman's shows, I want to talk to men about proper shot selection and the need to use the right equipment to efficiently kill an elk, but most guys blow me off with their own ramblings about some new gadget that is supposed to take the place of all that stuff that I want to talk about. And then they go out and do something dumb, and the end result is another dirty little secret about a wounded elk.

The best way to kill an elk is to study the animal's anatomy, learn where the vital organs are located, and then determine where an arrow must be placed to humanely kill an elk with an arrow. Ultimately, there is only one position that an elk should be in when taking a shot, but there are several questionable and downright bad shot options. Learn these things, and you will kill every elk you shoot.

Elk Anatomy

An elk is a big-boned, heavily-muscled animal with an elongated body that resembles a deer, but an elk is much larger in size, with a

The best way to become proficient at making killing shots on bull elk is to first study the elk's anatomy – learn where the vital organs are located along with its massive bone structure – before you take that shot.

mature bull weighing anywhere from 800 to 1,000 pounds. There are some good things and bad things about an elk's size. The killing zone on an elk is much larger than a deer because an elk's chest is about thirty-six inches from top of shoulder to bottom of chest. There is about twelve inches below the back that is dead space, plus about six inches from the bottom of the chest upwards. That leaves a vertical target of eighteen inches. The elk's lungs extend from in front of the shoulder, about twenty-four inches back, with the liver plastered right against them, separated by the thin diaphragm muscle. That affords about eighteen inches horizontally from the line behind the back of the shoulder back to the liver. In other words, an archer has a vital target eighteen inches by eighteen inches to shoot at. Most archers, whether shooting precise high tech gear or traditional equipment, can hit an eighteen-inch bullseye at thirty yards, and certainly at twenty yards, and it's automatic at ten yards. Right? Wrong! For a variety of reasons, most of which are avoidable, too many bowhunters fail to penetrate this large vital area on an elk, even at close range.

One of the biggest problem areas on an elk's anatomy is the shoulder blade. Most archers are mainly deer hunters and have learned to aim as a deer's chest where the back of the foreleg meets the center of the chest. This is necessary because a deer's chest presents a small target, with most of the lungs hidden behind the shoulder. A broadhead that hits the relatively thin shoulder blade of a deer has no trouble slicing through it.

On an elk, it's a far different matter. The weight of an elk tends to push down the shoulder blade, forcing it behind the leg farther to the rear. That means that any archer who aims at a bull's chest directly above the back of the foreleg, will hit the shoulder blade. An elk's shoulder bone is much larger and more massive than a deer's, and this mass is fully capable of stopping a broadhead shot from a lightweight bow, especially if that broadhead contains multiple heads that offer excessive resistance.

Where to Aim at an Elk

Because of the problem with the shoulder blade extending back beyond the foreleg, you should aim at the center of the bull's chest and about six inches behind that imaginary line made by the back of the foreleg. At best, your arrow will hit the elk's ribcage, and it doesn't take a lot of kinetic energy to drive an efficient broadhead through the thin ribcage and into the lung area. At worst, a shot a bit forward will clip the thin edge of the shoulder blade, which doesn't offer much resistance. If you hit a bit farther back, you'll still catch the back of the lungs or the liver.

The shoulder hit, with the shoulder blade stopping penetration of the broadhead before it can slice into a vital organ, is responsible for the vast majority of bowshot elk that are not retrieved. Try as we might to avoid it, a shoulder hit is going to occasionally happen, but there is no reason why that elk should not be killed. A two-blade cutting edge broadhead offers very little resistance when it impacts the shoulder blade of an elk, and it easily slices through the flat, plate-like bone.

On the other hand, a multi-blade broadhead with a chisel or round point offers much more resistance upon impact with the shoulder blade, and if the kinetic energy is insufficient to drive the multi-blade head through the shoulder blade, the result is a wounded elk that may or may not live, but who will probably not be retrieved because it will go a long way before succumbing, if at all.

Even worse than a multi-blade broadhead is an expandable blade (mechanical) head. These heads were developed because of the paranoia among high-tech archers for pinpoint accuracy. Their bows and accessories are so sensitive that it's almost impossible to fine tune this equipment, resulting in poor arrow flight. To counter this, many archers

The perfect shot at a bull elk is a standing broadside shot at close range.

have been misled into believing that the compact, field-point type appearance of a mechanical broadhead will give them better accuracy.

What mechanical broadhead users are not being told is that upwards to 30% or more of the arrow's energy is used just to open the blades on an expandable blade broadhead. Is it any wonder, then, that many of these blades fail to penetrate far enough into an elk's chest to kill it? (And why in the heck have a three-inch wide cutting surface?) Add to the above problems the mechanical broadhead's tendency to cartwheel and flip the arrow sideways as the blades begin to expand when quartering into a game animal, and you have a broadhead made in hell for bigger game.

So poor has been the performance of these expandable blade broadheads on elk that some outfitters, and especially those who specialize in larger game, won't allow their clients to use them.

The Perfect Elk Shot

As I mentioned at the beginning of this chapter, I was responsible for the two retrieved elk out of thirteen shot during a two year period. The first bull was a record class six-point shot standing broadside at eighteen yards. The second bull was a five-point shot standing broadside at twelve yards. Of the nine that were wounded and lost, nine were shot at between thirty-five and sixty-five yards, and the other two were shot at under twenty yards while they were moving.

In my opinion, the perfect shot at an elk is offered when a bull is standing broadside at close range. There are three criteria in the previous statement: Standing, Broadside, Close Range. I demand all three before I shoot, and you should, too. Remove any one of the above and you may still kill the elk, but a margin of error is introduced that has the potential to ruin the shot. Remove any two of the above, and your potential to ruin the shot increases greatly. Remove all three of the above, and you are a fool if you shoot. Let's examine these three criteria.

Broadside. The lungs should be the focal point of your shot. Take out the lungs, and the elk dies quickly. I realize that a heart shot kills quickly also, as does a liver hit, though more slowly. But these organs are too small and obscure to seriously try to hit them when taking a shot. The lungs, on the other hand, are the largest vital organs and take up most of the ribcage. An arrow that penetrates just twelve inches into the ribcage of a broadside elk is going to slice into both lungs.

Standing. An archer needs time to stabilize and aim his bow and arrow. Too many things must line up before an accurate shot can be

Avoid trying to force an arrow through brush and limbs at an elk.

made, be it with a compound bow or a long bow. Elk move at a fast clip – seven miles per hour or more – and that's way too fast to be shooting at one. It's easy to stop a moving elk. Just cow call, or smack your lips, or whistle – anything to stop the elk.

And here's a note of warning. Don't rely on your guide to stop the elk for you. Many guides are college kids who are looking for part time work until they start fall classes. They have little or no elk savvy, and it probably wouldn't occur to them to stop your elk so you could get a standing shot. To assure that the bull stops when you are ready to shoot, be prepared to stop it yourself. But be ready to shoot when that elk stops because he will quickly size up the situation, identify the danger, and bolt.

Close Range. Discussion of proper range reminds me of the debate over pornography. Whenever an effort is made to ban pornography, somebody jumps up and screams, "Who are you to tell me what I should or shouldn't read or look at! And then we bemoan the insidious deterioration of our country's morals.

Same thing with the issue of proper range. Whenever I make a comment about proper range, someone jumps up and screams, "Who are you to tell me at what range I should be shooting!" And then we bemoan the lack of responsible shots being taken. It's gotten so bad that even bowhunting magazines allow hotshot writers to tout long range shooting in excess of fifty yards, with the apologetic philosophy: Everybody shoots according to their ability. That thinking, of course, means that some guys can shoot better than others. Let me state that, after almost fifty years shooting and watching the best archers in the world shoot under hunting conditions, no one should be shooting beyond forty yards.

My range is thirty yards and under (and the closer the better). The reason is simple: No matter how much we hop up archery gear, the arrow remains a very slow moving projectile, affected by the vagaries of wind, rain, atmosphere, gravity, to say nothing of the movement of the game from the flight path before the arrow gets there. Case in point, there is not a bow made that shoots an arrow fast enough to avoid missing an alert deer before it jumps the string. I'm an engineer; I've already calculated it for a *Bowhunter Magazine* article, and it's not even close.

Shots To Avoid

You should avoid taking these five shots: long shot, frontal shot, quartering frontal shot, quartering away shot, rear shot. None of these shots hold much promise for the archer, and they are the primary culprits,

Avoid the long shot and the quartering forward shot. Neither afford a good chance of making a killing shot.

along with poor judgment on the shooter's part, why an elk is shot and not killed.

Long Shot. I picked the long shot first because some archers, I won't call them bowhunters, brag that they are able to kill game beyond fifty yards consistently. They may have gotten lucky and managed to hit something out that far once or twice, and that's all they can remember. A few years ago, I watched a man who was the vice president of a large bow manufacturing company shoot at an elk target in elk camp. The man's shooting was truly remarkable; he routinely made shots out to eighty yards, and he never did bother with anything under fifty yards. He should have. He got a shot at a five-point bull at thirty-five yards and hit it back in the loins – a miss of about four feet. Target range accuracy and hunting accuracy are totally different. Don't fall into the trap, while shooting at your range in the summer, of flattering yourself into believing that you are one of those modern reincarnations of Howard Hill. Keep your shots at forty yards and under, and you won't have any "dirty little secrets" to keep you awake at night.

Frontal Shot. A man, well known in archery circles, sent me a video of a bull elk he killed, hoping I'd use it in one of my elk hunting videos and thereby make him famous. The video shows the man cow calling, and a big bull stomping forward, but the bull stops at thirty yards because the guy's set-up is exposed. The bull offers only a frontal shot. To my horror, the guy shoots the elk square in the center of the chest. The video goes on to show the guy finding the elk, which may be accurate. I wrote him a terse letter explaining that we do not allow anything in our videos that is illegal, unethical or irresponsible, and the frontal shot he took was irresponsible because there is too much muscle and bone protecting the lungs and heart. Yes, the guy probably did kill that bull, but I have a host of sad tales of wounded elk running off with an arrow sticking out the front of their chests. A frontal shot is a poor choice; it's a stupid choice. Pass it up and go home with a clear conscience.

Quartering Frontal Shot. The quartering frontal shot, in some ways, is even worse than the frontal shot. At least with the frontal shot, the arrow is usually stopped before it penetrates deep enough to mortally wound the elk. With the quartering shot, enough damage may be done to cause the elk to die long after the hunter has returned home. Here's why. There is just enough of the ribcage showing on a quartering frontal shot to tempt a weak-minded bowhunter to try to slip the arrow into the ribcage. However, the ribs almost always deflect the arrow, sending it

The quartering away shot should also be avoided because the ribcage or shoulder blade may send the arrow off course or even stop its penetration. The frontal shot, rear shot and neck shot should never be taken.

instead into the paunch and intestines. That's not enough to kill the bull quickly, and since such a wound bleeds little, the elk almost always runs off and eventually dies of peritonitis in some thicket far from where it was shot.

Quartering Away Shot. Some bowhunters argue that this is an ethical shot, but I disagree. So does the PBS (Professional Bowhunters Society). The problem with the quartering away shot, again, is that an arrow that strikes the ribcage at an angle is often deflected along the rib bones, and the arrow ends up lodged in the bull's shoulder. I've documented seven instances when arrows were found inside a rifle-killed bull's body along the ribcage, or in the shoulder area (Plus two in the loin area from quartering frontal shots). Great for public relations, huh?

One of these elk was a huge 400 class nontypical bull that was rifle-killed during the 2002 season by Isaiah Jones in the Selway River country of Idaho. Isaiah found the front half of an aluminum arrow encased in gristle in the massive bull's shoulder. Yes, an elk can be killed with a quartering away shot, but an elk can also be wounded. Why take a chance of wounding the elk? Why not wait for the elk to turn broadside, or wait for another day?

Rear Shot. A few years ago, I would have thought it unnecessary to even have to mention the folly of taking a rear shot, but I have since read an expert bowhunter comment in a bowhunting magazine that the rear ham shot is a decent shot to take because of the massive hemorrhaging that takes place when all that muscle is sliced into.

Nonsense. No, madness! What could that man have been thinking of, to put in print such a dangerous and irresponsible statement? An arrow that hits the rear of an elk is stopped by the hip or leg bone. The only chance for a quick death from a rear hit, albeit a slim one, is if the femoral artery is cut. Conversely, I've heard several stories about idiots who took a rear shot and never found the wounded animal. With this ilk, though, the only remorse is that they lost an expensive arrow. Such a person wouldn't give a thought to the pain and suffering caused to an elk, nor would they lose a minute's sleep over the misery their dim-wittedness caused.

Target range accuracy requires mental and physical control. Same thing with in-field hunting accuracy, but ethical control (common sense) must also be added to the hunting accuracy equation because it is not styrofoam we are shooting at, but flesh and blood.

The best way to find your bowshot elk is to shoot it standing broadside at close range, and it will not run far enough to even have to follow a blood trail.

Chapter 14

SOLVING THE PROBLEM OF FINDING
YOUR BOW-SHOT ELK

My wife, Aggie, and I recently visited our friend, Laura Miller, who has a passion for jigsaw puzzles. Laura will dump one of those thousand-piece puzzles onto the table and painstakingly fashion a beautiful picture out of the jumble of pieces by using meticulous procedures learned from years of experience. On the day we visited, Laura had just completed a large Thomas Kincaide puzzle. The scene was of an English country cottage, aglow as only Thomas Kincaide can paint it.

In spite of the beautiful scene, I couldn't help but criticize it. "Laura," I commented with some degree of consternation, "it's nice, but it's not finished." I pointed to the center of the puzzle where the English cottage was located and stated the obvious, "You're missing a piece." Surrounded by an intricately woven mosaic of puzzle pieces was a hole.

"I couldn't finish it," Laura groaned. "I looked all over the place, but there's a piece to the puzzle missing." We all stood back and, try as we might, that intricate jigsaw puzzle was, and would always be, unfinished without that last piece fitting into place.

It's the same way with an elk hunt. Like gathering the pieces of a large jigsaw puzzle, a hunter must choose the proper archery gear and practice with it, get in good physical condition, find a good area to hunt elk and then find prime elk habitat, locate rutting bulls, use the right calling and hunting tactics to get that bull coming forward, and finally set up a good ambush before taking the proper shot.

At this point, the elk hunting puzzle is almost complete. All the pieces have fit together as tightly and beautifully as that Thomas

Kincaide puzzle. But if you can't find your bow-shot elk, your entire hunt will resemble a puzzle with a piece missing. It will remain incomplete, no matter how much you try to rationalize it. You left the most important piece of the elk hunting puzzle out.

I don't want that to ever happen to you, and it won't, if you pay special attention to Chapters 12 (Ambush Setup), Chapter 13 (Shot Selection), and this chapter (Finding Your Bow-shot Elk). No matter how you look at it, this is the most important chapter in this book because it's the last piece of the elk hunting puzzle.

The Best Way to Find Your Bow-shot Elk

The best way to find your bow-shot elk is to avoid following a blood trail. I know this sounds silly, but consider this: You take up the blood trail because you don't know where the animal is, and you follow a trail of crimson with the hope that a dead elk will be at the end of it. It's like following a rainbow, and that's not the way I like to do it, because rainbows disappear, and so do blood trails.

Here's a good example. You shoot an elk, and it runs off, leaving a copious blood trail, and you fully expect to find this elk. All you have to do is follow the numerous spots of crimson to the elk. Then the clouds build and the wind blows and the rain pours down. Your blood trail – that vital link between you and your elk – is washed away. Now what are you going to do to find your elk? My suggestion, at this point, would be prayer.

That's why I don't like to follow a blood trail. The point I am trying to make here is this: If you hit an elk when he is standing broadside at close range (see Chapter 13), you will probably see or hear the elk go down. And here's the proof of that statement. Of the forty elk I've killed, I had to follow a blood trail only six times to retrieve the elk. The other thirty-four elk went down either in my sight, or close enough that I heard the elk fall. It was a simple matter of walking up to the animal and claiming it.

Elk are big animals. They make a lot of noise when they run. Even in open terrain, you'll be able to follow the flight of a bow-shot elk because they make so darn much racket when they gallop away. An elk shot through both lungs is not going to make it much farther than a hundred yards, and most don't even make it that far. So even if you don't see or hear the elk go down, by following the sound of the elk, you'll have a pretty good idea where he is lying because I've learned through the years that the spot where I last heard the elk running is usually the spot where he quit moving and died.

It's as simple as that when you shoot an elk standing broadside at close range. When you don't, you pay the consequence. Many times, I've helped other hunters search for their bow-shot elk, crawling on our hands and knees searching for infrequent specks of blood. At some point during this physically and emotionally tortuous experience, the hunter would lament, " I wish I could have that arrow back. I wish I'd never taken that shot."

The Four Types of Wounds

In a perfect world, the elk are always standing broadside at close range, but life – and the hunt – are not always perfect. Things happen during those tense moments when an elk is in range. The possibility of an off-target hit remains a constant possibility. An unseen branch could also send the arrow off course, or the elk may bolt at the last second. When these unforseen things happen, the arrow may hit the elk in a place that does not bring about a quick death. That doesn't mean the elk won't die; it just means that it's run off beyond hearing and seeing range. In other words, you really don't know where it is, so you have the trail of blood to it.

The chest shot produces the vast majority of quick elk kills because it causes massive hemorrhaging and collapses the lungs.

There are four types of wounds that an arrow can inflict upon an elk, ranging from a mortal wound that results in a quick death, to a flesh wound that will heal and leave the elk no worse for the wear. By examining these four types of wounds, we can better understand how to analyze a hit and retrieve that bow-shot animal.

Short Term Mortal Wound

An arrow that slices through both lungs will kill an elk within seconds. It's what every bowhunter should strive for, and the kind of hit that you are almost guaranteed to make if the elk is standing broadside at close range. After the arrow hits the elk and slices through both lungs, massive hemorrhaging occurs. In addition, the lungs, which are under pressure, quickly collapse, rendering them incapable of sending life-giving oxygen to the brain. Think about it. If your lungs went out with no warning, you'd be on the floor within seconds. That's exactly what happens to a bull elk after you double-lung him. He runs off, usually unaware of exactly what had just happened. Once out of sight he stops, coughs to clear his lungs (because they are rapidly filling with blood), stumbles because he is feeling light-headed (no oxygen is finding its way to his brain), and then he collapses.

After I shoot an elk, even with a perfect standing broadside shot, I immediately note where the elk was standing when I shot him, and the very last place I saw the elk before he disappeared. That furnishes a direct line of flight and will provide valuable aid if I must take up the blood trail. After the bull is out of sight, I listen to him crashing off, and note when and where he stops running, then I listen for the telltale cough. I've heard this cough in roughly half the bow-shot elk I've killed. In heavy cover, you'll hear the elk crash to the ground, but if the animal is standing seventy yards away in an aspen grove, you may not hear him fall. However, it's been my experience that the place where you heard him cough is the place where you'll find him.

If you're not sure if your elk was hit in the lungs, examine the blood. It should be bright red with tiny air bubbles in it, to a frothy pink in color. Even if you've never seen lung blood before, the first time you look at it and see all those tiny air bubbles, you'll recognize that it came from the lungs. Because the lungs are under pressure, the blood trail from a lung-shot elk will often show up, not only on the ground, but also high up on bushes and trees, as a red spray.

Of course, a low hit in the chest may slice into the heart. If that happens, bright red blood will be sprayed everywhere, and the animal

An arrow that strikes the shoulder blade of an elk may penetrate deep enough to slice into the near lung, but not far enough to catch the far lung. This elk will run off and bed down and die, but the bowhunter should wait for about an hour to allow the animal to bleed out.

will drop quickly.

Medium Term Mortal Wound

An arrow that strikes the shoulder blade of a bull may penetrate deep enough to slice into the near lung, but not far enough to catch the far lung. This type of wound is mortal, but the elk may not die within seconds, as it would have if both lungs had been taken out.

An elk that is shot in one lung will run off. This burst of activity creates an overload to his cardiopulmonary system, because the one lung is rapidly filling with blood and losing its pressure, and then shock sets in. The elk will run about a hundred yards and begin to feel lightheaded and sick. Being unaware of exactly what happened, he will not be overly alarmed and will bed down. And if you don't get impatient and push him out of his bed, he'll die there within an hour.

Three of the elk that I've blood trailed were shot in one lung. I could tell that the arrow had probably not penetrated deep enough to catch the far lung, so I listened to the elk run away. I then sat down and waited about an hour. (That's why most experts suggest you wait for an hour. It's not for the double-lunged animal. It's for those marginal hits that require the animal to bleed out.) Then I walk over to the last place I saw the elk. That's when I take up the blood trail, which should be copious because it was a lung hit. With all three elk, I located the animal about a hundred yards away, lying in a bedded position, which meant that the elk felt sick, then bedded in the tucked leg position before expiring.

A hit farther back in the chest will catch the end of the lungs, or it may hit the liver. A liver hit can result in an elk's death within minutes, or it may take an hour, depending on the damage done to this major blood-filtering organ. I once shot an elk far back in the ribcage, and it ran off about seventy yards and stopped in view. I watched the elk stand there looking around, then its head dropped and it stood that way for about a minute, then it bedded down. By the time I got to it, the bull was dead. Total time was not more than five minutes.

Expect the blood from a liver hit to be rich red, with no air bubbles. And don't expect the blood trail to be a spray, as with the lungs, which are under pressure. The blood trail from a liver hit will be copious, splashing onto the ground in a steady stream.

Long-Term Mortal Wound

An arrow that hits behind the ribcage has probably missed all the elk's vital organs. This is often called a paunch hit, or gut shot, because the arrow sliced into the belly or intestines. An elk usually dies from this wound, but it takes a long time, and since no vital organs were hit to shut down the elk's system, the animal has the capacity to run a long ways. And because that part of the elk's anatomy does not contain many blood vessels, the blood trail will be very light.

This elk will eventually die from peritonitis, a septic condition that occurs when bacteria from the food in its belly is introduced into the antiseptic parts of the body, causing death. A gut shot elk can live up to twenty-four hours or more, but after about twelve hours it will often be too weak to rise out of its bed. A gut-shot elk is a bowhunter's worst nightmare. You know the elk is going to die, but you also know it is capable of running a long distance, and there will be very little blood.

The good news is that the elk will probably run off a few hundred yards, feel sick, and bed down in cover. The elk may stay there and die, or it may get up and move several times during its torment. The bad news is that if you leave that elk lying there overnight, chances are great that the meat will be spoiled in the morning. But if you take up the blood trail too soon, you could very possibly make matters worse by kicking the sick animal out of its bed, and a spooked elk, even a sick one, can go a mile or more in just a few minutes.

My advice on a gut-shot elk is to base your decision, to follow it or not, on the time of day you shot it. If the elk was shot early in the morning, he will have had ten hours to stiffen up while the peritonitis raged in his system, and you might want to try to find him that last hour or two in the evening. If the bull was shot in the evening, you might be smart to leave the elk alone and wait until morning. If the elk doesn't die too quickly overnight, the meat will probably still be good.

This is a very difficult decision to make, with no guarantees that the blood trail will even be heavy enough to follow. Several times, I've been asked to help find gut-shot elk, and more often than not, we lost the blood trail before we found the elk.

The blood trail from a gut-shot elk is easily to identify. The blood will be dark red, with seeds and chewed up pieces of grass mixed with the blood. Just describing it makes me sick in my heart.

Some archers claim that a multi-blade broadhead is better than a two blade broadhead on elk because the multiple blades create more of a blood trail. That is nonsense. Any hit on an elk in a non-vital area is not going to bleed very well because there aren't many blood vessels in the paunch area. Of course, an arrow shot into the rear hams will leave more of a blood trail, but that elk will run five miles before it stops.

An arrow that hits behind the ribcage will miss the vital organs, but will probably still kill the elk if the paunch is hit because peritonitis will eventually set in, but it may take upwards to 24 hours for the bull to die.

Non-Mortal Wound

An elk that is hit high in the back, or in the butt, or in the shoulder, or neck, or low in the ribcage will probably live because no vital organs were hit, and no food matter was introduced into the system. But you don't know that, so you should search for the elk for at least a day. Even though the arrow appeared off target, it could have nicked the back of the liver before entering the paunch or hit the spleen; the arrow could have severed the femoral artery when it hit the butt; the arrow may have nicked or severed the jugular vein if it hit the neck; it could have sliced into the major artery running under the backbone if it hit high.

There are times when it is obvious that the hit is non-mortal. A shoulder hit, when the arrow is stopped after penetrating an inch or two, and bounces out or flops down as the elk runs away, is not going to kill that elk. Neither will a hit high in the neck, or low in the leg. But if there is any possibility that the elk may have been mortally wounded, use the rest of the day looking for it. That's the least you can do for the animal.

Writing about non-mortal hits troubles my spirit. I have flashbacks to instances when I've gone out to help other bowhunters who were beside themselves with anguish and guilt because they'd taken a shot that they shouldn't have. They not only lost their trophy, but they also wasted valuable hunting time while alerting other elk to their presence.

It's discouraging, as I follow a sparse blood trail uphill. (A mortally wounded elk rarely goes uphill.). I know we will not find this animal. The anguished bowhunter wrings his hands and says, in so many words, "Oh great elk hunter, work your magic." And there's nothing I can do to help him get his elk. I am, after all, only human, possessing neither clairvoyant powers nor extrasensory perception. My ability to find bow-shot game depends on three criteria: an elk (1)standing (2)broadside at (3)close range before it is shot. I am a master at finding these kinds of bow-shot elk.

Additional Blood Trailing Tips

•Mark with a plastic pink or orange ribbon the spot where the elk was standing when hit, and the last place you saw it before it disappeared.

•Find the blood at the second ribbon and analyze it for lung hit, liver hit, etc.

•Mark every ten feet of blood trail with a piece of ribbon. If you lose the blood trail momentarily, step back and sight down the ribbon line to get an accurate "line of flight" of the animal. Go forward to that point and begin searching for the blood trail again.

    •If the blood trail is lost, look ahead for an area of cover where a wounded animal might seek refuge.

If you haven't killed many (or any) bull elk, and a Pope & Young sized bull like this one is beneath your standards, maybe you need to reassess your penchant for phallic symbols.

Chapter 15

THE PHILOSOPHY OF ELK HUNTING TODAY

A new breed of sportsman has emerged on the hunting scene in the last decade. One of them stopped by my home in Montana recently. The young man quickly explained that his passion was bowhunting, and though only twenty-two, he was determined to compile an impressive array of trophy big game animals. He specifically wanted a big bull and asked if I'd killed any big elk.

I had a hunch what he was after, but I replied, "All my elk are big, would you like to see some of my racks?"

We went out to my garage, and the young man casually passed by several five-point elk racks, plus two six-point racks. He paused in front of a six-point rack that I'd scored high enough to make the Pope & Young Record Book.

"Is that one big enough for you?" I asked.

The young man stood there, studying the rack for a full minute before he shook his head and commented, "Not really."

"A 280 point bull isn't big enough for your first elk?"

The features in his face now stern and resolute, the young man announced, "I want my first bull to be a Booner."

There you have it, the new breed of sportsman in America, who knows nothing about the elk and how to hunt it, and cares even less about its wonderful habitat. He just wants his first bull elk to qualify for the Boone & Crockett Club Record Book, meaning a minimum score of 365 points.

I see and hear this extreme trophy hunting philosophy espoused more and more, and I'm not exactly sure how we got to this point in the sporting world, where the size and dimensions of an animal are the driving force behind the hunt.

The ego-driven desire for trophy antlers has led men lacking morals to break game laws and even sneak into Yellowstone National Park to poach trophy sized bulls.

Outdoor magazines, I suspicion, are the primary culprits Their pages often include misleading advertising by manufacturers who tout their wares with all the subtlety of a cruise missile: Buy our product, and you, too, can kill the biggest bulls and bucks. And as a plethora of manufacturers vie for sportsmen's dollars, these messages become more and more outrageous, like the bow manufacturer's advertisement that shows a high powered rifle bullet with fletching on the case, and the claim, "It's that fast!"

Some of the ads even strive to appeal to a man's prurient nature, like the one showing a scantily clad woman shooting a bow, with the subliminal message: "Be a real man and shoot this equipment – and you'll not only get the big bucks, but you'll also get me." Indeed!

Many of these advertisements are silly and easily shrugged off by us hype-conscious experienced archers, but they are read seriously by the new generation of archers who have been brought up in a society increasingly dependent, and expectant, on a quick fix for everything. A society where cyberspace has created an impatience in mankind to demand everything now, with money being the cure for everything – including hunting success.

I have tried to buck this troubling trend, with little success. Editors demand articles about how to kill the biggest bucks and bulls. I recently sent a letter to the editor of an archery magazine proposing an article about hunting elk late in the rut. The editor wrote back that the article idea sounded fine, but he wanted me to concentrate on how to kill the big bulls, not just Pope & Young, but Booners. I informed him that I'd never killed a Boone & Crockett bull, not even close. He wrote back and said maybe I wasn't the guy to write the article. This, from a man who'd killed only one bull elk in his life!

Not all of today's archery magazines are like the above publication. *Bowhunter Magazine* editor, Dwight Schuh, recently asked me to write an article about shooting does. Dwight explained, "We get a lot of letters from guys who complain that they hunt where you can't hardly even find a buck, let alone a 160 class buck. They want to know why I don't ever do anything about the excitement of shooting a deer, and forget about the rack on its head. So I wrote the article, with the title, "Doe Hunting as a Lifestyle." The article centered around the joy of the hunt, and the role that the hunter plays in the cycle of nature.

Dwight is extremely rare in his capacity as an editor. Not only is he sensitive to the real world of hunting on public land far removed from the game farm hunts and lucrative private land hunts, but he also practices what he preaches. On his last hunt, he took up the long bow and killed a cow elk, and he considers the feat a noble accomplishment.

My window into the world of misplaced morals and blind ambition that has seeped into the commercial world of archery hunting began when I was assigned to write an expose' for *Bowhunter Magazine* about Don Lewis, a bowhunter who was caught poaching mule deer in Utah. Authorities found in Lewis' possession a videotape that they traced back to Yellowstone National Park. Lewis and a cohort had been sneaking into the Park and killing massive (uh, shall we call them "trophy") size bull elk. Authorities couldn't be sure how many bulls were illegally killed, but estimates range upwards to a dozen.

The impact of that number hit me like a rock. A dozen bull elk were killed for nothing more than their antlers. The meat was left to rot. Lewis, who was a rising star in the archery world, claimed that manufacturers put pressure on him to produce bigger racks for advertisement purposes. We can disqualify Lewis' statements as self-serving rationalizing, but his sordid example of success at any cost is not alone. Other well-known, so-called trophy hunters have been purged from both the Boone & Crockett Club and Pope & Young Club when it was discovered that their trophies were either taken illegally or unethically.

At the root of every one of these atrocities is a sordid tale of greed and gluttony and self aggrandizement, where prowess in the hunt is equated to the size of the horns or antlers displayed on a wall. To the point where men are driven to sneak into Yellowstone, of all places, and kill half-tame elk so they can be looked upon as special. At least Don Lewis poached his animals with a bow. Other men have rifle killed elk and then claimed them as bow kills. All they needed was an accomplice to swear to their lie on the Pope & Young Record Book application, and they're in!

All this rhetoric about the evils of trophy hunting may lead you to believe that I am against the pursuit of big bulls. I am not, and I would be a liar if I said I would not like to shoot a really big bull some day. My point is that the unrestrained drive to procure big antlers for the purpose of ego, cheapens the hunt and it cheapens the experience. To lower an elk to little more than a bowling trophy also cheapens the true value of the animal, for the bull elk is, in my opinion, one of the most majestic creatures that roams the earth.

Conversely, some trophy hunters disregard, to the point of disrespect, any elk that does not meet their preconceived notion of what a trophy bull should be. I got an earful from a disgusted outfitter one day at a large sportsman's show on the subject. The man recognized me and mentioned that I should write an article about, "all these guys who just want to kill big bulls.

"Last year I had a client who just about made me sick," the outfitter grumbled. "I was guiding this guy on a one-on-one bowhunt. All he wanted was a trophy bull. The guy'd never even killed an elk before, but he had to have a Boone & Crockett bull.

"I called in three different bulls, and one of 'em woulda made Pope & Young. I mean, I had these bulls standing in front of the guy at twenty yards and under. A blind man coulda killed 'em. But, oh no, he wouldn't think of it.

"So on the next to last day we got into this big herd bull and chased him for a mile before he holed up in some black timber. We sneaked in, but the bull got nervous and started to leave. I cow called, hoping to bring the bull back. He stopped at about seventy yards and bugled once. All we could see was the bull's ass. Next thing I know, the guy shoots! He hits the bull square in the ass and it runs off. I couldn't

Outfitters have related stories to me about trophy hunters with misplaced priorities who will pass up the perfect close range standing broadside shot at a decent bull elk because it was beneath their trophy standards, but then take an irresponsible long range or butt shot at a big bull.

believe it! I asked the guy what the hell he was shooting at, and he said the butt was the only shot he had, so he took it.

"We followed the bull for a long ways before the blood trail ran out. The guy just shrugged and wanted to know where some other big bulls like that one might be found."

The outfitter shook his head and summed up his gripe. "These guys'll pass up a decent bull at point blank range, then wing an arrow seventy yards at an elk's ass just for the chance to take home big horns. You tell me what sense that makes."

I had no answer for that man, and promised him I'd consider writing an article on the subject, though I already knew no outdoor magazine would be interested in such an article. But I was greatly disturbed by the man's story, and as I pondered it, I recalled another hunting story about an ass shot at an elk that I feel is worth relating.

Dale Burk, the owner of Stoneydale Press and publisher of this book, encountered a huge bull in an isolated basin in southwest Montana during the 2001 season. Dale told me it was the biggest bull he'd ever seen. This, coming from a man who's hunting career has spanned more than 50 years, with more than 40 elk to his credit. So I knew the elk must have been a monster.

Dale told me he first saw the bull in dense timber on the backside of the mountain and crept closer for a shot. The bull was unsure what Dale was, but the elk was also determined to not allow Dale to get closer. Hunter and hunted played a high-stakes game of cat and mouse, until Dale finally got the upper hand when the bull stopped in a small opening. Dale told me, "Oh, he was huge! I've never seen such antlers, even in the national parks."

The bull would have been a fitting trophy for a man who'd paid his dues and put in his time in the elk woods and had worked hard for scores of years just to get this chance of a lifetime to finally bring home a Boone & Crockett sized bull.

One tiny problem. The bull was quartering away, with only his huge rump sticking out. Dale waited and waited; man and trophy bull stood in tense silence for seconds, then minutes. And then the bull moved away. Twice more on succeeding hunts, Dale encountered the bull, but the elk, more wary than ever, offered Dale little more than a fleeting glimpse of those awesome antlers disappearing into the dark timber.

As Dale mulled over that fateful encounter, there were many facets of the hunt that he would have liked to change: Maybe a different approach here, or a few more cow calls there. But of one thing he remains adamant. That bull was too magnificent an animal to risk a poor shot. "There was no way I was going to rump shoot that beautiful animal. No elk is worth that to me. I just couldn't live with myself. I'll go back there next year and try for that bull again. Hopefully, he'll be there. If not, at least my conscience is clear."

The keyword in Dale's story is: CONSCIENCE. It's a term missing in much of today's society, and all too often in hunting circles. For the conscience takes over when laws fail to cover those murky areas of hunting that may not be illegal according to the game laws, but they most certainly are distasteful and unethical.

Game farms hunting is a good example of a hunter's need for a conscience. Driven by the need to come back with big horns or antlers, certain hunters have resorted to some very questionable tactics to bring home a trophy to brag about. In my home town of Superior, Montana, a local bar routinely purchased elk racks from locals, then turned around and sold them for hundreds of dollars to nonresident hunters, who took them home as trophies.

Buying an elk rack to take home was better than nothing, but it lacked the illusion of reality, especially when folks back home began asking to see the hide, or maybe taste a few elk steaks. Certain enterprising men began raising elk in pens, then offered "controlled hunts," which amounted to nothing more than shooting an elk in a pen. To you and me, such a scenario is so absurd that it's laughable. But they came. By the hundreds!

How, I wondered, could a person, in the name of sportsmanship, call himself a hunter and shoot an elk in an enclosure. It began to chew at me. What kind of man would do such a thing? And that led to even more questions: Who were these people ? Why would they want to hunt on a game farm, instead of in the beautiful elk woods?

Being a writer and journalist, I set out to answer these questions. I obtained a list of client references from a Montana game farm, proudly given to me by the owner. I began making phone calls. What I discovered was a microcosm of what is wrong today, not only with trophy hunting, but with our nation in general.

I interviewed twelve men, spanning all geographical areas of the country. The one common denominator these men possessed was money. A game farm hunt is expensive; you pay thousands of dollars, depending upon the size of the elk you kill. When a bull reaches trophy size, say 330 points, the price may reach upwards to ten thousand dollars.

For most of the men whom I interviewed, their main reason for hunting on a game farm was that it was just good business. Some had taken guided hunts in the past and either didn't get an elk, or they shot elk that were too small for them. So, being good businessmen and entrepreneurs, they maximized their profit margins. As one guy put it, "I really didn't care that the elk was standing in an enclosure when I shot it. If I'm going to spend ten grand, I want to get my money's worth."

My question, "Why would you hunt an elk in a pen?" caused most of these men to bristle. One man snapped, "The elk weren't in pens. That's what everybody thinks, that you just walk out and shoot a bull elk in a pen. In the place where I hunted, it looked just like woods. You couldn't hardly tell there was a fence around the place." Hmm!

When I informed that man that the elk he shot was born and raised on a farm five hundred miles away, he stammered, "I, uh, I wasn't aware of that. I thought they were born there and just lived in that patch of woods." But the man recovered quickly and replied, "Hey, this wasn't like shooting fish in a barrel. We (he hunted with a buddy) had to hunt our asses off to get our bulls. That enclosure was at least twenty acres, maybe more. I mean, you had to go in there and find an elk all by yourself. I finally caught a big six-pointer in a fence corner and shot him."

How could any hunter, in the name of sportsmanship, go to a game farm and kill a bull elk in a pen? How could you sleep at night?

Two bowhunters that I interviewed thought I was crazy to insinuate that what they were doing might be unethical. "Hey," one guy countered, "we hunted hard for our elk. A couple times, we had to ask the guide to push some of the bulls back into our corner of the enclosure. There were a lot of tense moments. When a couple thousand bucks rides on the size of the bull you shoot, you want to make damn sure of the animal you choose.

"One time I had this big seven point bull walk right up to me while I sat on the four-wheeler. I could have shot him at thirty feet, but the money they wanted for a 400 point bull was way too much for me. I finally settled for a six-pointer that scored 320 points."

But the saddest story came from a man who'd brought his fifteen- and sixteen-year old sons to a Montana game farm for their first gun hunt. "I didn't want them getting all discouraged and quitting hunting because they didn't get anything," the man explained, then added with a note of pride, "I wanted my boys to learn how to make a clean, killing shot."

The man went on to say, "Both boys made good shots. Killed their bulls the first day, shooting from a steady rest on the four-wheeler."

I wonder how many of these men went home and informed their families and hunting buddies that they went out to Montana and killed their elk in an enclosure? I would hazard to guess none of them. That question led to an even more disturbing one: How many of these men entered their elk racks in the Boone & Crockett and Pope & Young record books?

Forgive me for even thinking such a thing. These men might shoot their elk in a pen, but they'd surely never lie to family and friends about the circumstances of their kills, and certainly not to the venerable Boone & Crockett or Pope & Young Clubs, right?

In contrast to this disturbing trend among elk hunters is my son, Tony. After a bout of phone calls to guys who hunted game farms, Tony's philosophy on hunting is unique and refreshing. "I'm an elk hunter, Dad," he reminds me all the time. "The object of an elk hunt is to kill an elk. I'll kill anything that's legal if I feel like it. I just like being out there with the elk. I've killed enough bulls. I don't need any of this big-bull crap. If a big cow steps in front of me, and I get the urge, I'm gonna shoot her. And you know I will. I've done it before." Tony adds with a smirk, "That's why they call it elk hunting, and not bull elk hunting."

The large majority of hunters are like Tony, but it is that small

Tony Lapinski's philosophy on elk hunting is unique and refreshing. He loves the elk woods, loves the animals, and considers any elk, such as this cow, to be a worthy trophy.

percentage of ego-driven hunters who step over the line legally, ethically and morally who seem to garner the most attention – all of it bad. Unfortunately, this adverse publicity is what the public sees and hears most, and we must remember that it is the public who will ultimately form the "public opinion" about elk hunting, especially since most of it occurs on public lands. Therefore, a positive public opinion is critically important today because a major threat to elk hunting looms in the near future. Allow me to explain.

For decades, we hunters have rightly claimed that hunting is necessary to trim surplus deer and elk herds in the West. The animal rights people hated that argument because they had nothing to counter this truth.

The introduction of the wolf changed all that. The animal rights faction knew exactly what they were doing when they pushed hard for wolf reintroduction in Yellowstone National Park and Idaho. That was barely ten years ago. Already, wolf numbers are approaching 250 in Yellowstone, with another 260 in Idaho and 200 in Montana. Wolves are rapidly extending their range into Wyoming, with Colorado next in line. In the meantime, the Mexican wolf is slowly building in the Southwest, and it's only a matter of time before the pack takes up the hunt in earnest in New Mexico and Arizona. At least Washington and Oregon are safe, right? Wrong. Already, a wolf has swum the Snake River from Idaho into Oregon, and it's only a matter of time before hunting packs will be established in these states.

Deer are the favorite prey of wolves, but elk are a close second, and the Idaho wolves have proven that the biggest, fleetest elk is no match for a pack of cunning wolves. As the wolf population has exploded, elk numbers in some areas have dipped to the danger point, and in places such as the Paradise Valley north of Yellowstone, the calf crop is not surviving long enough to replenish the herd.

As elk numbers drop, their absence will be felt by their two main predators – man and wolf. I foresee this issue arriving on the desk of some federal judge, who will weigh the necessity of both sides. Should the wolves be allowed to take the elk for food? Or should sport hunters be allowed to kill the elk for trophies?

Can you see where I'm going with this trophy hunting /wolf issue? It is much larger than some hunter's big-horn ego or the wolf population overburdening the elk herds. Some federal judge, because of adverse publicity from a few slob hunters, is going to look at all hunters as wanting to kill elk just to rip off their heads and hang them on their

I believe that the best way to establish the sportsman's right to maintain his and her historic quest for game is to become as we once were – hunter/gatherers who pursue the elk as an integral part of the cycle of nature.

walls, and say, "Enough!"

My belief is that the best way to establish the sportsman's right to maintain his historic, noble quest for game is to become as we once were – hunter/gatherers. The animal rights faction finds little sympathy from the public when they complain about Indian and Eskimo peoples hunting to subsist.

The role of man as hunter/gatherer is historic; it's traditional, and it's ethically and biologically efficient. Killing an elk for the sole purpose of jerking its head off and hanging it on the wall, besides being repulsive to most people (including myself) is not. And yet, I know far too many men who hunt elk solely for bragging rights, with little or no regard for the large amount of healthy meat a mature elk provides. Heck, I know one guy who's trying to make a name for himself as a trophy elk hunter, who's been traipsing around the West killing on average three big bulls per year – and he's a vegetarian!

A man's right (and currently his privilege by law) is to hunt because of his age-old role as hunter/gatherer. If it should be decided in court that the purpose of the hunter is no longer to act as a supreme predator who sustains his life's blood through the blood of the animals he slays, what ethical and moral role is his endeavor playing? Please don't answer that it keeps taxidermists in business.

The hunter's current role, as viewed by public opinion polls, is precariously close to being construed as ethically and morally wrong, mostly due to bad publicity by a few. The sole reason we can still hunt on public lands is because it is legal. And with the wolf issue soon to rear its ugly head in federal court, all it would take is some federal judge to look upon the wolf as the true hunter/gather – and today's sportsman as an obsolete, grotesque stealer of dead heads – and he has the authority to wipe out the hunting privilege on 90% of the land where elk roam..

I have not arrived at my ambivalent stance toward trophy hunting because I haven't been able to kill big bulls. I have killed a half dozen record books bulls, and I've been invited to travel south and bowhunt on two Indian Reservations, whereupon I too, would have returned as one of those "trophy" hunters who killed a 380 point bull. You see, it doesn't take a good hunter to kill a big bull; it just takes a guy with enough money to afford a game farm hunt or a trip to the White River Apache Indian Reservation.

But more than that, I have always felt that it is unethical and immoral to kill an animal for sport, or for only its head. Yes, I experience the pulse-quickening rush of adrenalin during the hunt, but sport, it is not.

How can you explain away the taking of a life as sport? Instead, I see myself as a predator and human hunter/gatherer in the cycle of nature, for to place man outside the natural order is to admit to the animal rights faction that man is not needed. I am indeed needed in the cycle of nature, much more so than the wolf, because I hunt to fulfill my part in the cycle, while still possessing the intellect to limit my hunting and killing in response to game dynamics.

The wolf, on the other hand, is a killer. Not with malice; nature just made it that way. The wolf doesn't stop when only calves are available, or when the herd thins out, or when the game is at a disadvantage due to deep snow. We are learning, much to everyone's

To truly show that you care, become a steward of the elk and its habitat by joining the Rocky Mountain Elk Foundation, a non-profit organization whose 130,000 members have combined their money, time, effort and love for the animal into a powerful conservation effort, having set aside more than 3 million acres of wildlife habitat throughout America.

(except the old-timers) chagrin, that the wolf looks upon everything as food, be it a deer or elk, or a white faced Hereford, or a llama (wolves have recently killed a half dozen llamas in the Nine Mile Valley east of my home in western Montana.).

Should we condemn trophy hunting? That'll never happen, as long as some men are allowed to exhibit their prowess through the size of the elk rack they bring home. Instead, what's needed is for the large percentage of hunters in America, and elk hunters in particular, to take the lead in practicing stewardship toward the animals and the land they roam.

To do that on a personal basis, you should sit down in a quiet place and do some thinking about how the rest of the world views your hunting endeavors. The best way to portray the sportsman, in my opinion, is as a hunter/gatherer, as a caretaker of the land and its animals, as a steward who cares and nurtures this special place we call elk country.

We can also become stewards of elk country collectively by joining the Rocky Mountain Elk Foundation, who's goal is to conserve, restore and enhance natural elk habitat by promoting sound management of wild, free-roaming elk which may be hunted or otherwise enjoyed. The RMEF fosters cooperation among federal, state and private organizations and individuals in wildlife management and habitat conservation. It also educates its members and the "general public" (remember them?) about habitat conservation, the value of hunting, hunting ethics and wildlife management. The Rocky Mountain Elk Foundation is the antithesis of the game farm ilk and the ego-driven trophy hunter, for its 130,000 members have pooled their money, time, effort and love of the animal into a powerful conservation effort, having set aside more than 3 million acres of wildlife habitat throughout America.

I'm not much of a joiner, but I do belong to the Rocky Mountain Elk Foundation. Please consider joining me in this worthwhile endeavor by writing or calling:

Rocky Mountain Elk Foundation
2291 W. Broadway
Missoula, MT 59808-1813
1-800-CALL-ELK

LISTING OF BOOKS

Additional copies of **SOLVING ELK HUNTING PROBLEMS** *and many other of Stoneydale Press' books on outdoor recreation, big game hunting, or historical reminisces centered around the Northern Rocky Mountain region, are available at many book stores and sporting goods stores, or direct from Stoneydale Press. If you'd like more information, you can contact us by calling a Toll Free Number,* **1-800-735-7006,** *by writing the address at the bottom of the page, or contacting us on the Web at* www.stoneydale.com. *Here's a partial listing of some of the books that are available, including a grouping of Mike Lapinski's popular books.*

Other Books by Mike Lapinski

High Pressure Elk Hunting, *By Mike Lapinski. The latest book available on hunting elk that have become educated to the presence of more hunters working them. Lots of info on hunting these elk. 192 pages, many photographs, hardcover or softcover.*

Radical Elk Hunting Strategies, *By Mike Lapinski. Takes over where other books on early-season elk hunting leave off to give advice on what the hunter must do to adapt to changing conditions. 162 pages, 70 photographs.*

Western Hunting Guide, *By Mike Lapinski, the most thorough guide on hunting the western states available. A listing of where-to-go in the western states alone makes the book a valuable reference tool. 168 pages, softcover.*

The Elk Mystique, *by Mike Lapinski. Big format, all-color book, this is one of the most exquisite books ever presented in both text and photography on the wapiti, the American elk. Softcover, 144 pages.*

Self Defense For Nature Lovers, *by Mike Lapinski. From mountain lions to grizzly bears, and potentially deadly snakes and other wild critters, this book covers ways you can handle potentially dangerous situations to avoid serious outcomes. 144 pages, softcover.*

Seasonal Pro Trapping, *by Mike Lapinski. Tells you how you can make your part-time trapping efforts profitable. Covers the business part of trapping to presentation of the basic trapping techniques for the major fur species. Softcover, 150 pages.*

Historical Reminisces

Mule Tracks: The Last of The Story, *by Howard Copenhaver. In what he says will be the final book in his series, master storyteller Howard Copenhaver focuses on the zany and often unpredictable antics of his beloved mules. In addition to wit and humor, he includes plenty of instruction on how to train and develop mules into dependable mountain stock. 176 pages, both hardcover and softcover.*

Copenhaver Country, *By Howard Copenhaver, the latest collection of humorous stories. Contains rich humor and studied observations of a land Howard loves and the people he met along the way in a lifetime spent in the wilds. 160 pages, many* *photographs.*

They Left Their Tracks, *By Howard Copenhaver, Recollections of Sixty Years as a Wilderness Outfitter, 192 pages, clothbound or softcover editions (One of our all-time most popular books.)*

More Tracks, *By Howard Copenhaver, 78 Years of Mountains, People & Happiness, 180 pages, clothbound or softcover editions.*

Indian Trails & Grizzly Tales, *By Bud Cheff Sr., 212 pages, available in clothbound and softcover editions.*

70,000 Miles Horseback In The Wilds of Idaho, *By Don Habel. Don Habel worked as an outfitter in the Idaho wilderness for more than forty years and has put together a wonderfully detailed and sensitive, as well as occasionally humorous, reminisce of his adventures in the wilds. 180 pages, softcover.*

The Potts' Factor Versus Murphy's Law, *By Stan Potts. Life story of famous Idaho outfitter Stan Potts, lots of photographs. 192 pages.*

Mules & Mountains, *By Margie E. Hahn, the story of Walt Hahn, Forest Service Packer, 164 pages, clothbound or softcover editions.*

Dreams Across The Divide: *Stories of the Montana Pioneers, Edited by Linda Wostrel, Foreword by Stephen Ambrose. Stories and photos of the first pioneers to settle in Montana. 448 pages.*

Another Man's Gold: A Novel of the Life & Times of James B. Stuart in Early Montana, *By Rod Johnson. Cattle drives, gold panning, rustlers, hangings, battles with outlaws feature this story of one of Montana's first settlers.*

Hunting Books

Bugling for Elk, *By Dwight Schuh, the bible on hunting early-season elk. A recognized classic, 164 pages, softcover edition only.*

A Hunt For the Great Northern, *By Herb Neils. This acclaimed new novel utilizes the drama of a hunting camp as the setting for a novel of intrigue, mystery, adventure and great challenge set in the woods of northwestern Montana. 204 pages, softcover.*

Ghost of The Wilderness, *By James "Mac" Mackee. A dramatic story of the pursuit of the mountain lion, the Ghost of The Wilderness. A tremendous tale of what Jim MacKee went through over several seasons in his quest for a trophy mountain lion in the wilds of Montana. 160 pages, softcover.*

The Woodsman And His Hatchet, *By Bud Cheff. Subtitled "Eighty Years on Wilderness Survival," this book gives you practical, common sense advice on survival under emergency conditions in the wilderness. Softcover.*

Memoirs of An Idaho Elk Hunter, *By Jens Andersen. This big book captures the vitality and romance of a lifetime spent hunting elk in Idaho and Montana. A superb read, many color photographs and illustrations. 216 pages, hardcover only.*

Coyote Hunting, *By Phil Simonski. Presents basics on hunting coyotes as well as caring for the pelts, 126 pages, many photographs, softcover only.*

Elk Hunting in the Northern Rockies, *By Ed Wolff. Uses expertise of five recognized elk hunting experts to show the five basic concepts used to hunt elk. Another of our very popular books, 162 pages, many photographs.*

So You Really Want To Be a Guide, By Dan Cherry. *The latest and single most authoritative source on what it takes to be a guide today. This book is an excellent guideline to a successful guiding career. Softcover edition only.*

Hunting Open Country Mule Deer, By Dwight Schuh. *Simply the best and most detailed book ever done for getting in close to big mule deer. The ultimate mule deer book by a recognized master, 14 chapters, 180 pages.*

Taking Big Bucks, By Ed Wolff. *Subtitled "Solving the Whitetail Riddle, " this book presents advice from top whitetail experts with an emphasis on hunting western whitetails. 176 pages, 62 photographs.*

Quest for Giant Bighorns, By Duncan Gilchrist. *Comprehensive overview on hunting bighorn sheep everywhere they're hunted; detailed how-to, where-to with lots of photos. 224 pages, softcover.*

Quest for Dall Rams, By Duncan Gilchrist. *The best source book ever put together on the beautiful Dall sheep, it's crammed with solid how-to and where-to information on hunting Dall sheep. 224 pages, 88 photographs, many charts, softcover format.*

Montana–Land of Giant Rams, Vol. III, By Duncan Gilchrist. *The best source and most acclaimed book available on hunting bighorn sheep in Montana. Updated and expanded from his earlier volumes on the same subject. 224 pages, many photographs, softcover format.*

Successful Big Game Hunting, By Duncan Gilchrist. *For more than four decades now, Duncan Gilchrist has hunted across North America as well as in Africa and New Zealand. This book touches every aspect of what it takes to be a successful hunter. 176 pages, 82 photographs, both softcover and hardcover formats.*

Field Care Handbook, By Duncan Gilchrist and Bill Sager. *The most comprehensive field guide available for the care of big game, birds, fish and other species. Illustrated by many of Duncan's photographs taken in the field. 168 pages, many photographs and illustrations, comb binding so it will lay flat while you use it.*

Cookbooks

Camp Cookbook, Featuring Recipes for Fixing Both at Home and in Camp, With Field Stories by Dale A. Burk, 216 pages, comb binding.

That Perfect Batch: The Hows and Whys of Making Sausage and Jerky, By Clem Stechelin. *Detailed instruction on techniques of making sausage and jerky at home from wild game, beef, etc. 116 pages, many photographs, comb binding.*

Cooking on Location, By Cheri Eby. *Exhaustive content for cooking on location in the outdoors, from menu planning to camp organization, meal preparation, and recipes for all sorts and styles of dishes. 139 pages, color photos and illustrations, comb binding.*

Venison As You Like It, By Ned Dobson. *A manual on getting the most from game meat, with over 200 recipes and instructions on using a variety of cooking methods.*

STONEYDALE PRESS PUBLISHING COMPANY

523 Main Street • Box 188
Stevensville, Montana 59870
Phone: 406-777-2729
Website: www.stoneydale.com